GW01336037

.....VOGGY S RECORDER SONGBOOK

This book belongs to:

....

Conception and manuscript: Martina Holtz
Composition (90): Martina Holtz
Lyrics (Page 17, 76): Martina Holtz

Cover design and illustrations: OZ, Essen (Katrin & Christian Brackmann)

© 2003 Voggenreiter Publishers
Viktoriastr. 25, D-53173 Bonn/Germany
www.voggenreiter.de
info@voggenreiter.de

ISBN: 3-8024-0465-3

Preface

Hello and welcome to my Recorder Songbook!

In this book I've collected some of the most beautiful and most popular songs for recorder for you. This book can be used as a supplement to Voggy's Recorder Book or with any other recorder-school. This is not a book for absolute beginners; to get the most out of it, you should at least have mastered the basics of the recorder and be able to read traditional notation.

I've tried to sort the songs according to topics, so you can hopefully find a suitable song for most occasions. There's also an alphabetical songlist at the end of the book.

Voggy

In this book you'll encounter two notes that aren't explained in Voggy's Recorder Book: the note F# (F sharp) and the note Bb (B flat). You'll find them both explained, together with their fingering diagrams, in the appendix of this book. As an additional hint, our little Voggy holds up a "warning sign" if one of these notes is needed to play a particular song. This way, you can look them up in the appendix, should the need arise. Some other helpful things you'll find in the appendix are:

- a table of the notes and their values,
- the most important meters (two of them; 2/4 meter and 6/8 meter are new for all of those who learned with Voggy's Recorder Book; you'll find them explained on p. 104).
- and fingering charts

so all the information you need is right at hand.
And now: have lots of fun!
Martina Holtz

Contents

Funny Tunes

Camptown Races

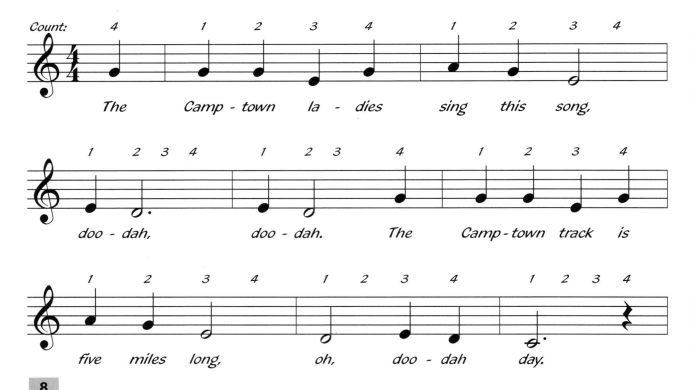

Hickory Dickory Dock

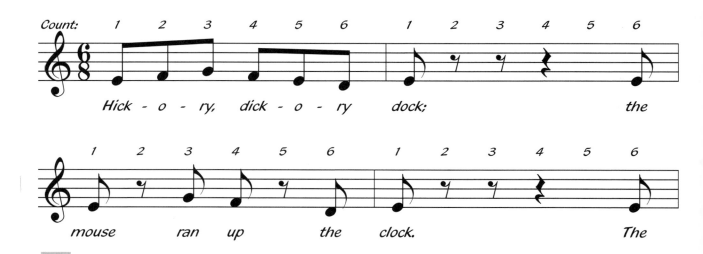

Jack and Jill

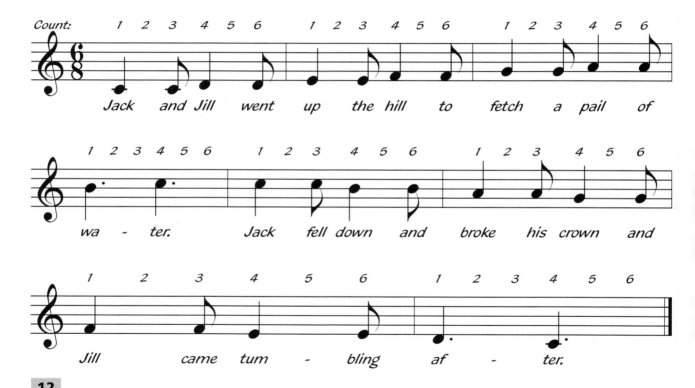

Skip to My Lou

J. J. J. Schmidt

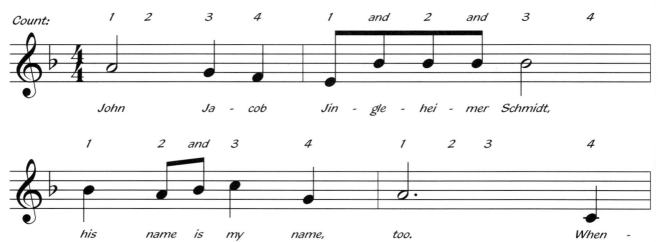

ev - er we go out, the peo - ple al - ways shout:

"John Ja - cob Jin - gle - hei - mer Schmidt!" La - la - La - La - La - La - La.

There's a Hole in the Bucket

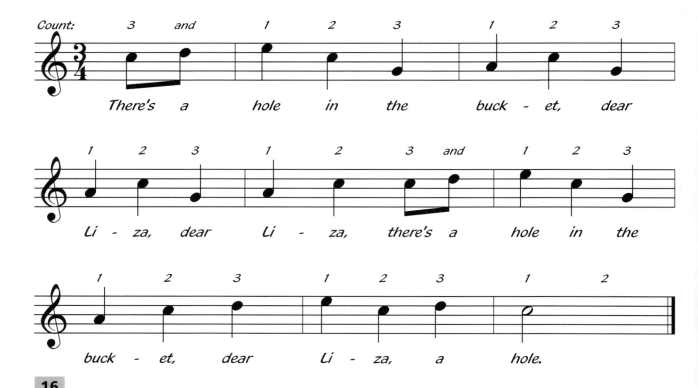

Once a Man

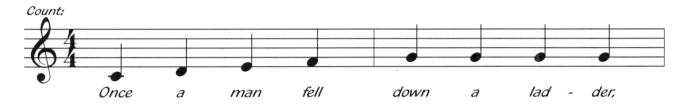

Once a man fell down a lad - der,

went to see the doc - tor. If he had - n't

fal - len down, he would - n't need a doc - tor.

Yankee Doodle

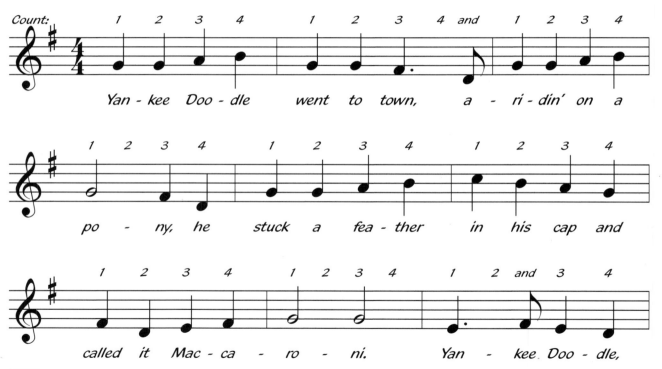

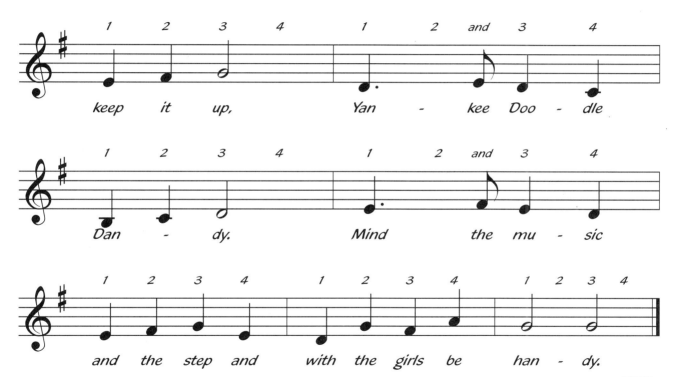

99 Bottles

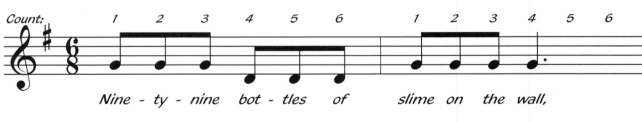

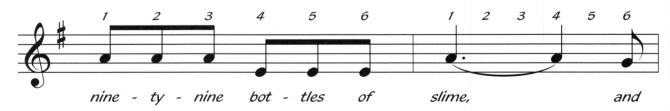

Polly Wolly Doodle

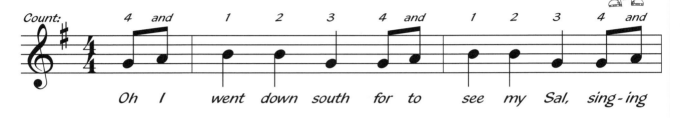

Count: 4 and | 1 2 3 4 and | 1 2 3 4 and

Oh I went down south for to see my Sal, sing-ing

1 and 2 and 3 and 4 and | 1 2 3 4 and

pol - ly wol - ly doo - dle all the day. My

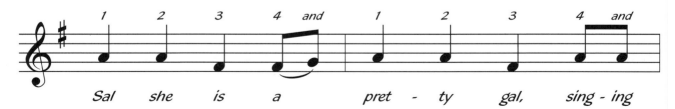

1 2 3 4 and | 1 2 3 4 and

Sal she is a pret - ty gal, sing - ing

Mixed Bag

A Tisket, a Tasket

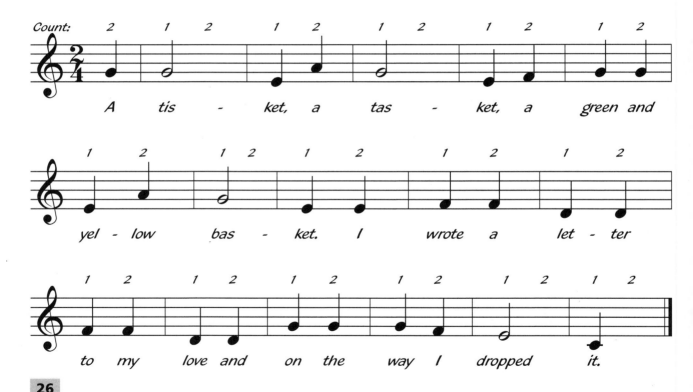

Amazing Grace

Clementine

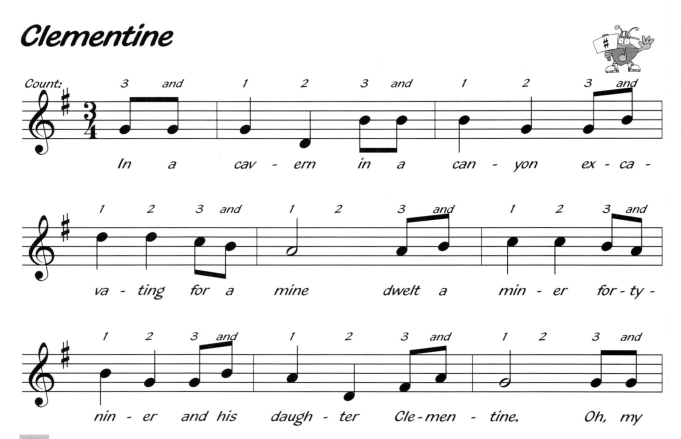

29

Down by the Station

Lavender's Blue

Count: 1   2   3   1   2   and   3   and   1   2   3

La - ven - der's   blue,   dil - ly,   dil - ly,   La - ven - der's

1   2   3   1   2   3   1   2   and   3   and

green;   when   I   am   King,   dil - ly,   dil - ly,

1   2   3   1   2   3   1   2   3   1   2   and   3   and

you   shall   be   queen.   Who   told   you   so,   dil - ly,   dil - ly,

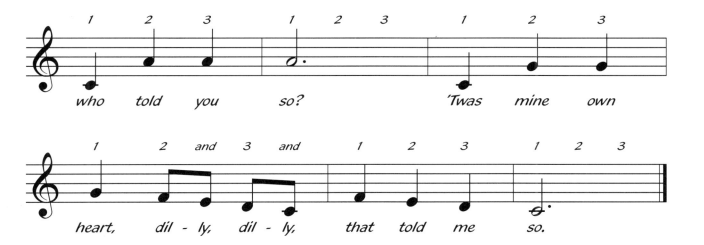

who told you so? 'Twas mine own

heart, dil - ly, dil - ly, that told me so.

33

He's Got the Whole World

London Bridge Is Falling Down

Rain, Rain, Go Away

Marianne

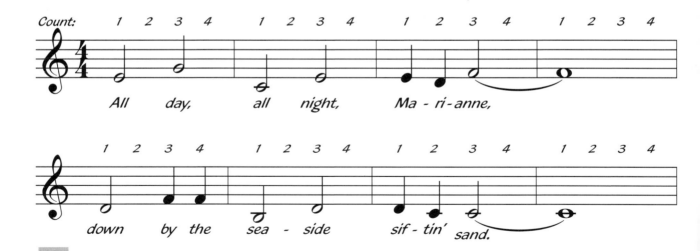

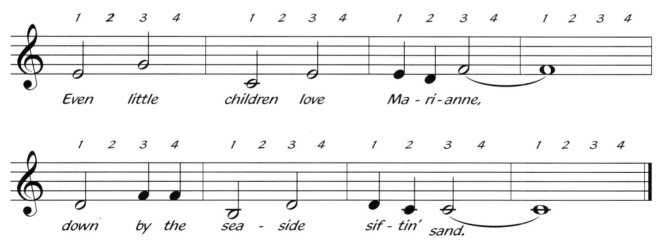

Even little children love Ma - ri - anne,

down by the sea - side sif - tin' sand.

My Bonny Is Over the Ocean

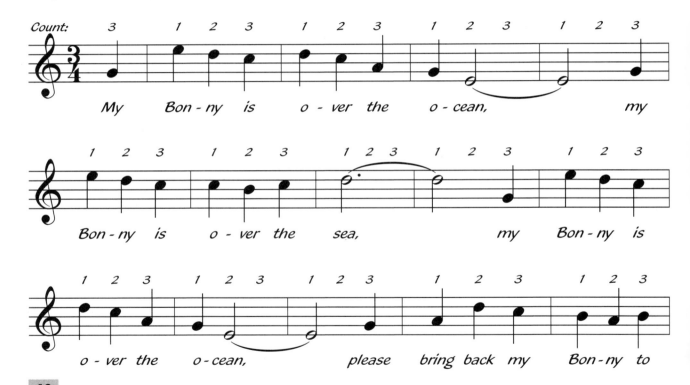

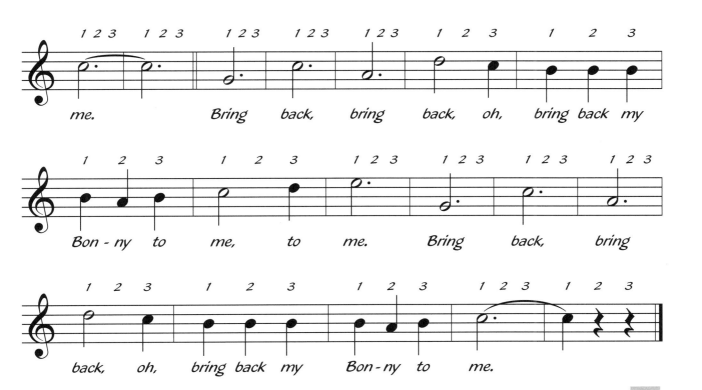

When the Saints Go Marchin' In

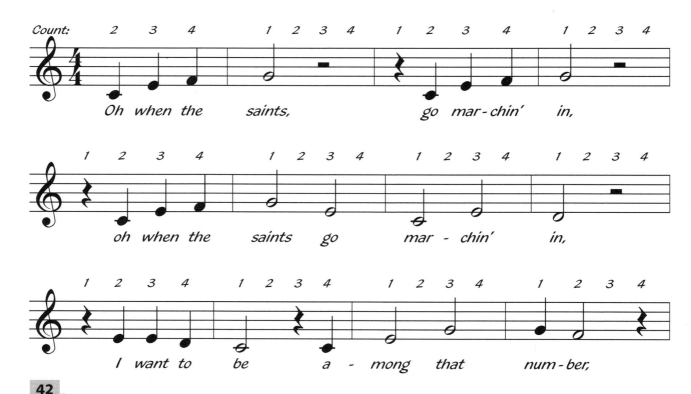

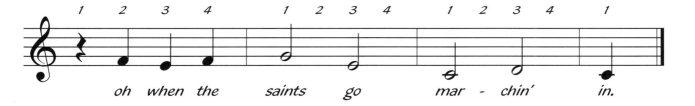

oh when the saints go mar - chin' in.

She'll Be Comin' Round the Mountain

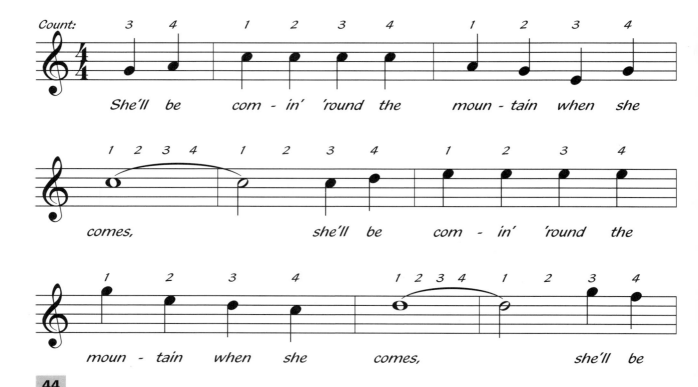

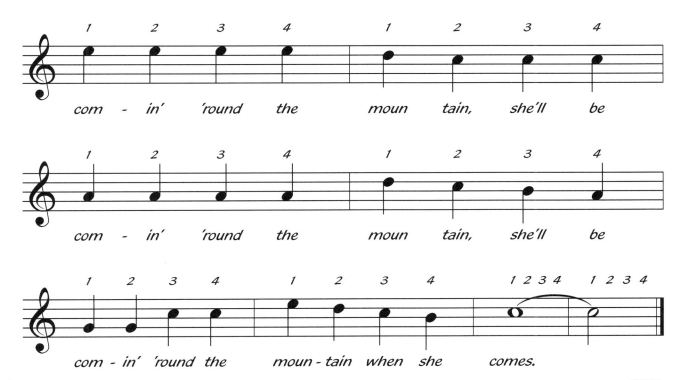

45

This Little Light of Mine

Count: 1 2 and 3 4   1 2 3 4   1 2 and 3 4   1 2 3 4

This lit - tle light of mine,   I'm gon - na let it shine.

This lit - tle light of mine,   I'm gon - na let it shine.

This lit - tle light of mine,   I'm gon-na let it shine, let it

shine, let it shine, let it shine.

If You're Happy

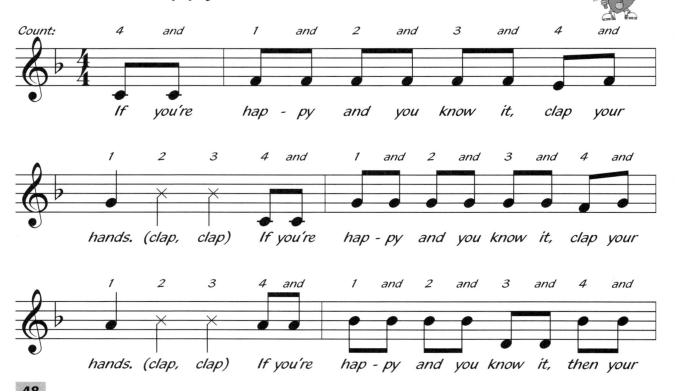

48

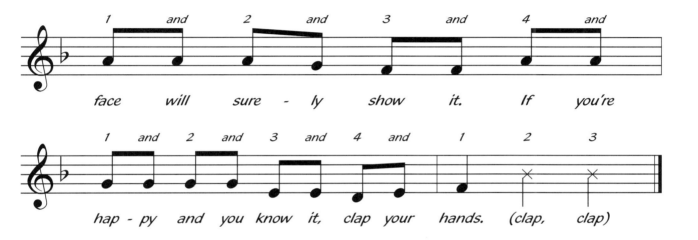

Oh Susanna

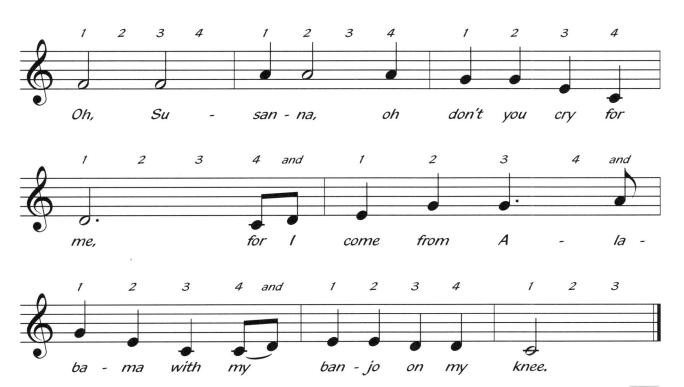

Can Can (Offenbach)

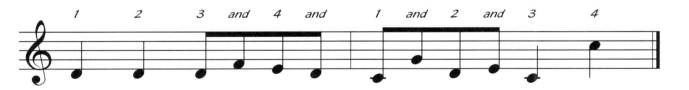

Row, Row, Row

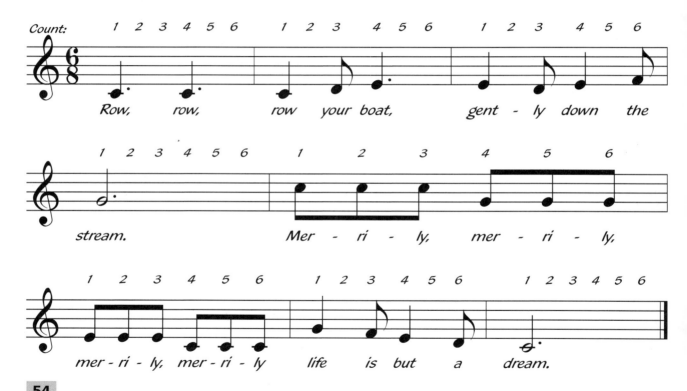

Michael, Row The Boat Ashore

55

Kum ba yah

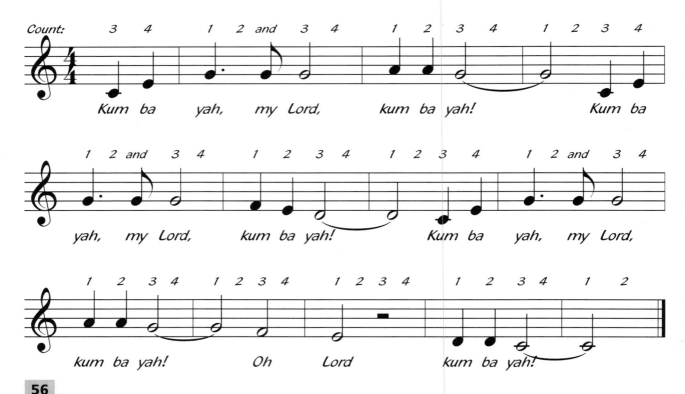

Men and Animals

Baa, Baa, Black Sheep

Count: 1 2 3 4 1 2 3 4

Baa, baa, black sheep, have you a - ny wool?

1 2 3 4 1 2 3 4 1 2 3 4

Yes sir, yes sir, three bags full. One for the mas - ter and

2 3 4 2 3 4

one for the dame, and one for the lit - tle boy that

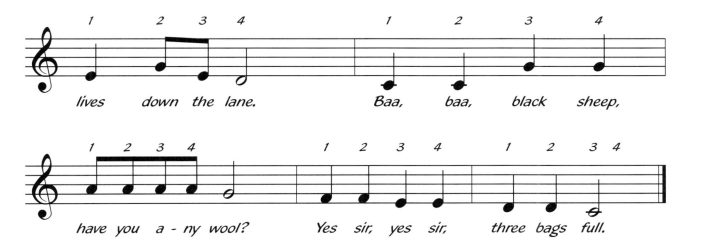

Bingo

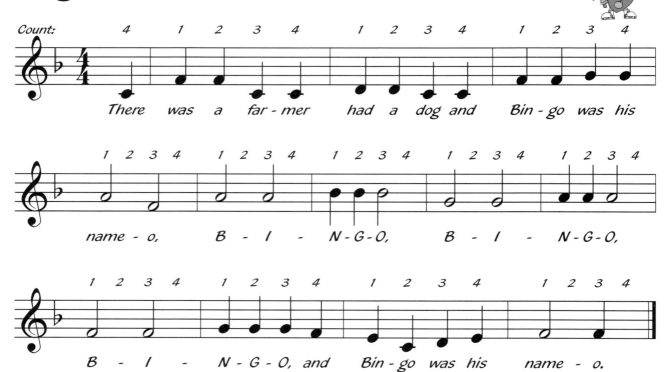

Pop Goes the Weasel

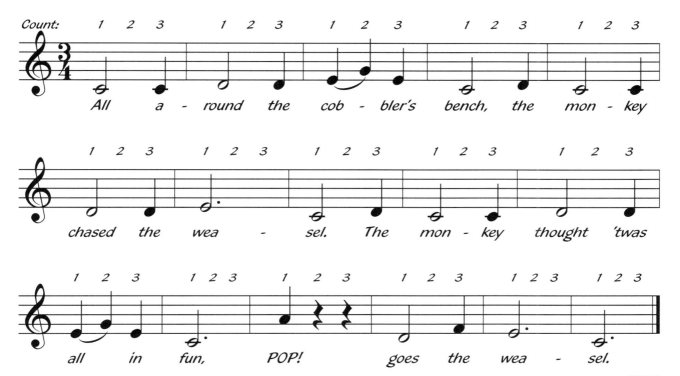

Count: 1 2 3   1 2 3   1 2 3   1 2 3   1 2 3

All   a - round   the   cob - bler's   bench,   the   mon - key

1 2 3   1 2 3   1 2 3   1 2 3   1 2 3

chased   the   wea   -   sel.   The   mon - key   thought   'twas

1 2 3   1 2 3   1 2 3   1 2 3   1 2 3   1 2 3

all   in   fun,   POP!   goes   the   wea   -   sel.

Teddy Bear

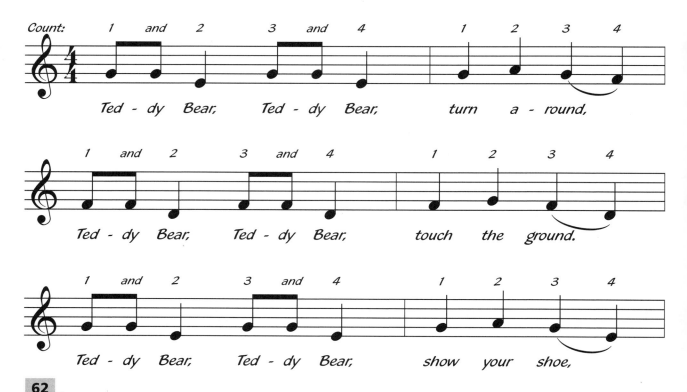

Crawdad Song

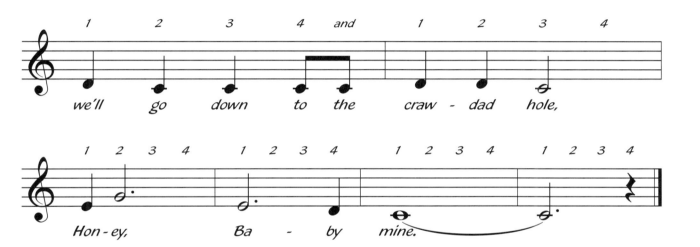

Eentsy, Weentsy Spider

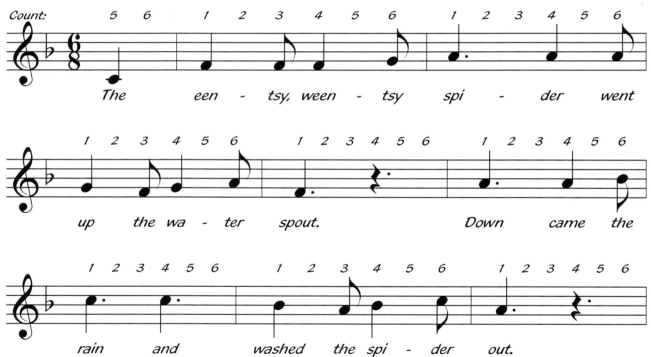

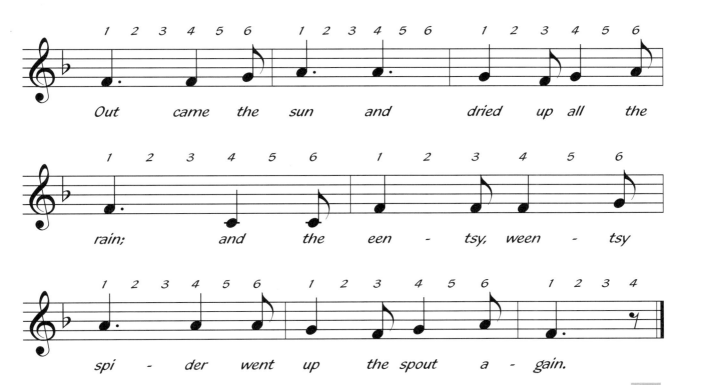

Hey, Diddle, Diddle

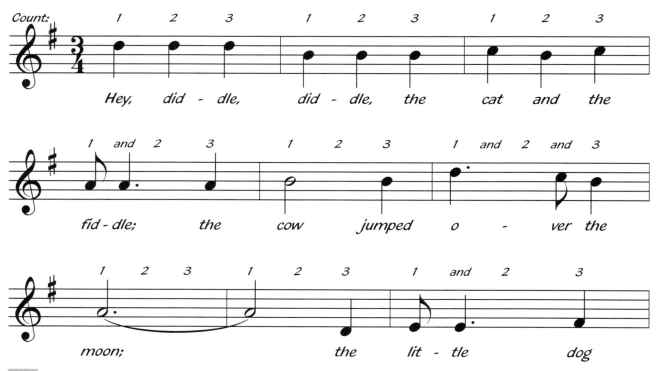

Count: 1   2   3   1   2   3   1   2   3

Hey,   did - dle,   did - dle,   the   cat   and   the

1 and 2   3   1   2   3   1 and 2 and 3

fid - dle;   the   cow   jumped   o   -   ver   the

1   2   3   1   2   3   1 and 2   3

moon;   the   lit - tle   dog

laughed   to   see   such   fun   and   the

dish ran a - way with the   spoon.

Little Green Frog

frog one day, and his eyes went "aah, aah, gung."

Old McDonald Had a Farm

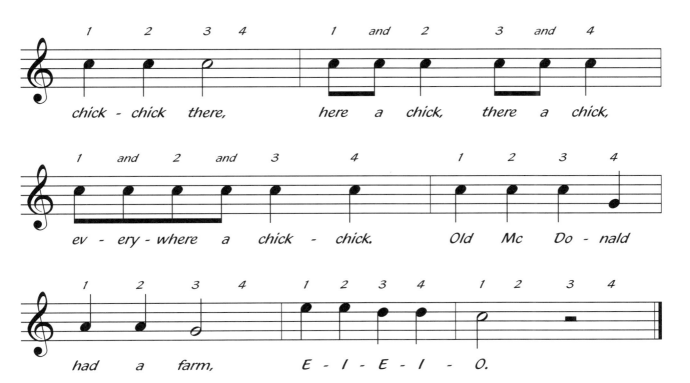

73

This Old Man

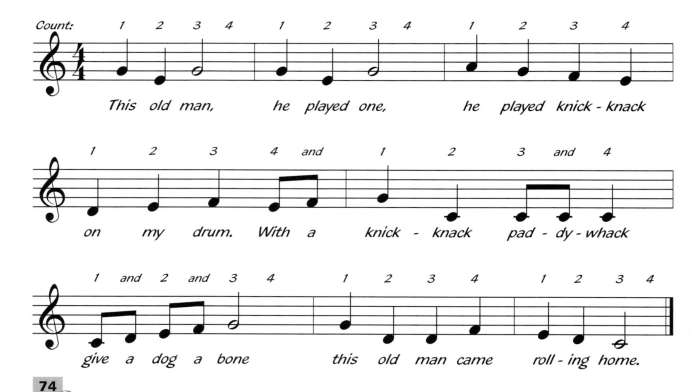

One Elephant Went Out

75

It's Raining

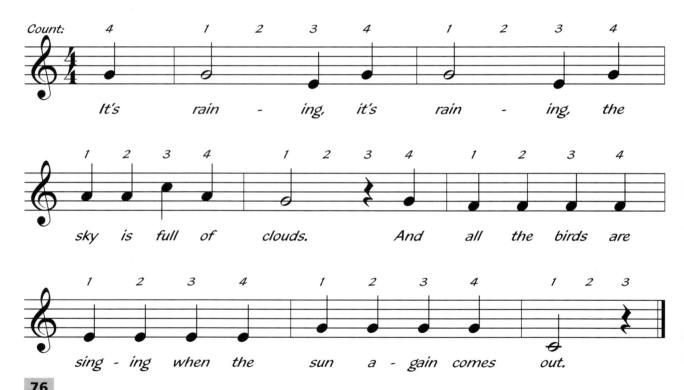

Count: 4 | 1 2 3 4 | 1 2 3 4

It's   rain - ing,   it's   rain - ing,   the

1 2 3 4 | 1 2 3 4 | 1 2 3 4

sky   is   full   of   clouds.   And   all   the   birds   are

1 2 3 4 | 1 2 3 4 | 1 2 3

sing - ing   when   the   sun   a - gain   comes   out.

76

Going to Bed and Waking Up

Brahms' Lullaby

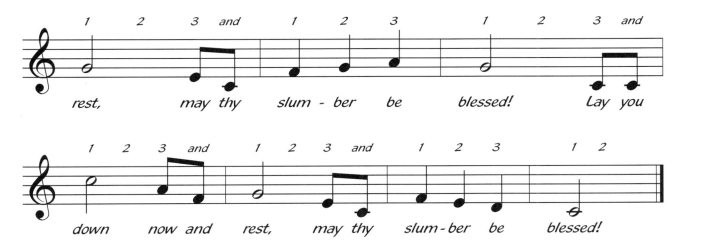

Hush-a-Bye, Baby

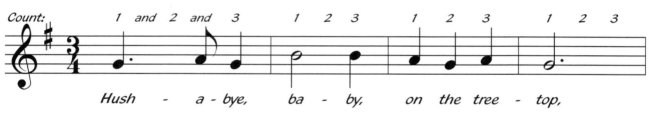

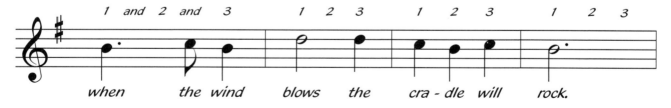

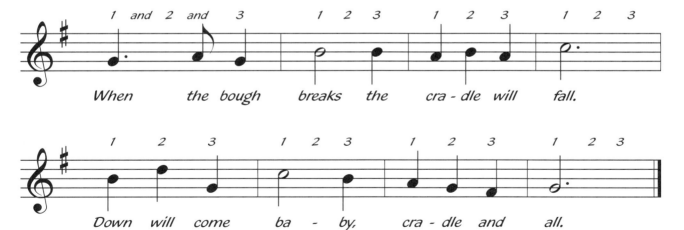

Brother John

Count: 1 2 3 4   1 2 3 4   1 2 3 4

Are you sleep-ing? Are you sleep-ing? Bro-ther John,

1 2 3 4   1 and 2 and 3 4

Bro-ther John. Morn-ing bells are ring - ing!

1 and 2 and 3 4   1 2 3 4   1 2 3 4

Morn-ing bells are ring-ing! Ding, Dang, Dong. Ding, Dang, Dong.

Good Morning

Goodnight Ladies

Count: 1 2 3 4 | 1 2 3 4 | 1 2 3 4 | 1 2 3 4

Good - night, La - dies! Good - night, La - dies!

1 2 3 4 | 1 2 3 4 | 1 and 2 3 4

Good - night, La - dies, we're go - ing to leave you

1 2 3 4 | 1 2 3 4 | 1 2 3 4

now. Mer - ri - ly we roll a - long,

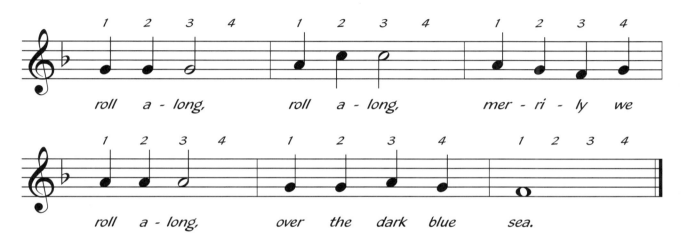

roll   a - long,   roll   a - long,   mer - ri - ly   we

roll   a - long,   over   the   dark   blue   sea.

Twinkle, Twinkle, Little Star

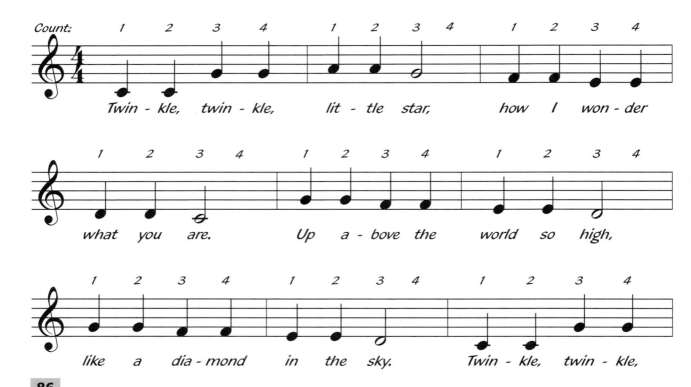

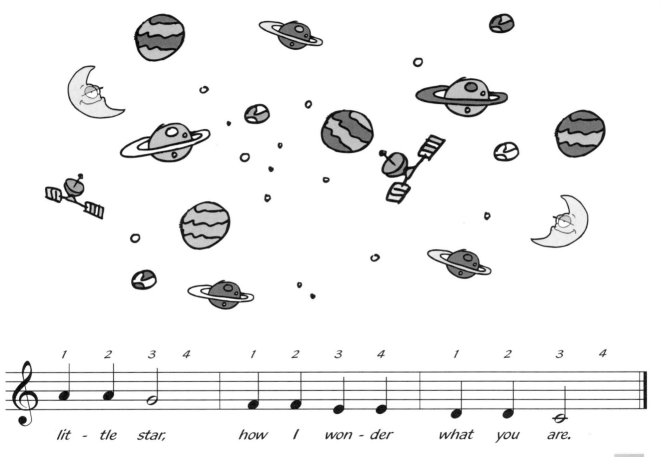

Hush, Little Baby

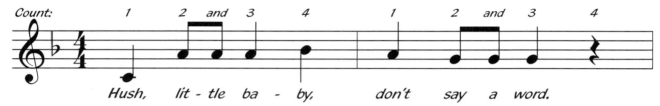

Sleep, Baby, Sleep

Count: 1 2 3 4   1 2 3 4   1 2 3 4

Sleep,   ba - by,   sleep.   Your   fa - ther   tends   the

sheep.   Your   moth - er   shakes   the   dream - land   tree,   down

falls a lit - tle   dream for thee.   Sleep,   ba - by,   sleep.

Sleep Tight

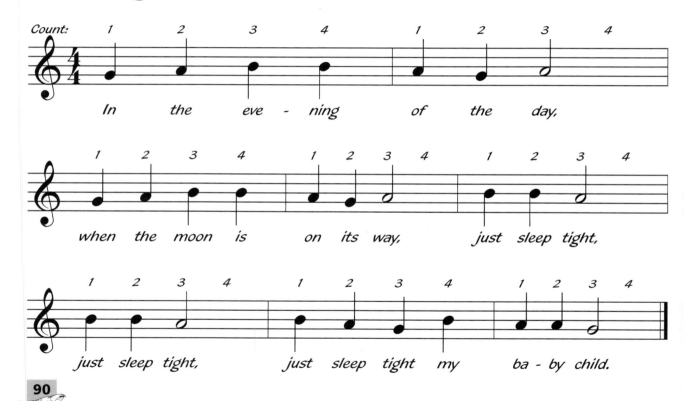

Christmas and Celebration

Jingle Bells

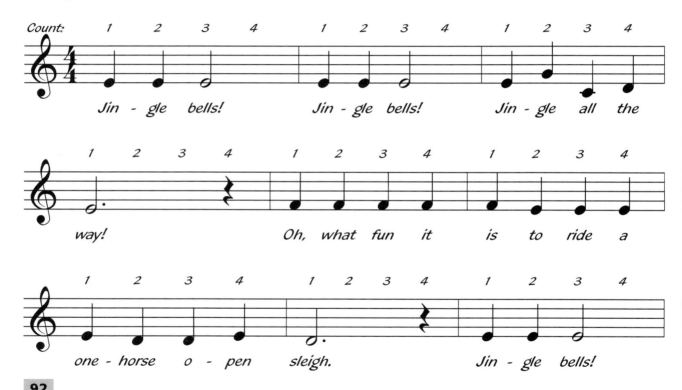

Silent Night

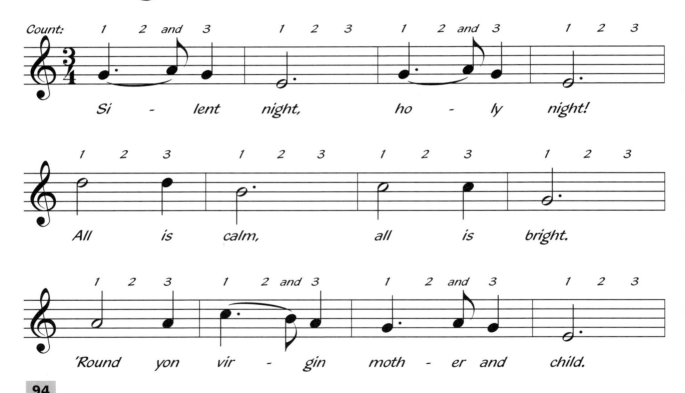

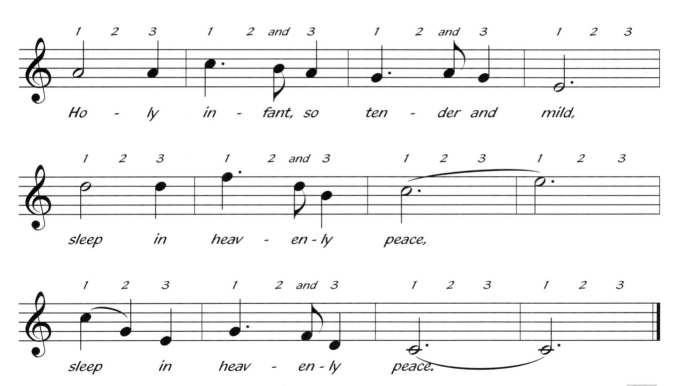

We Wish You a Merry Christmas

Jolly Good Fellow

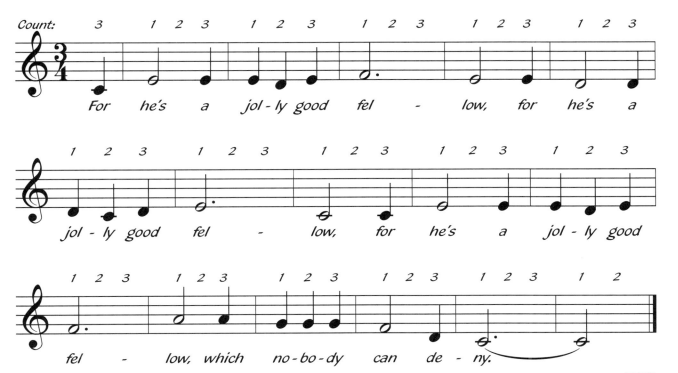

Ode to Joy (Beethoven)

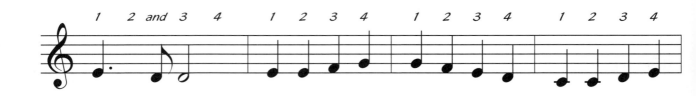

99

Caring For Your Recorder

To get the most out of your recorder and to ensure your instrument has a long life, you should do the following:

- After playing, disassemble your instrument and rub it gently with a soft cloth. Let the instrument dry a little. Wooden recorders don't like high temperatures, direct sunlight or very dry air. To prevent your recorder from cracking it should always be stored in pieces, and be assembled shortly before playing.

- Wooden recorders have to be oiled regularly about every two weeks (depending on their use) to protect them from moisture. Use **only** oil recommended by your local music store! Also, let them show you which parts of your instrument to oil, as this is not the same for all recorders.

A Word About Practicing

No musician likes to practice but there are a few simple tricks in order to make practicing as interesting and pleasant as possible.

1. Never practice when you don't feel like it! If you have to force yourself to practice, then it would be better not to start. If you notice while practicing that your mind is wandering elsewhere, stop practicing immediately.

2. It's better to practice daily for 20 minutes than to do nothing for two weeks and then three hours in a row. It's more important to practice regularly than at length.

3. If your hands become painful while playing, or if you notice pain in your body, stop immediately because your posture is probably cramped. Playing the recorder properly should never be painful.

Meter

To play the songs in this book, you'll need to know four meters: 4/4 meter (say "four-four meter" or "four-four time") 2/4 meter, 3/4 meter and 6/8 meter (say "six-eight meter" or "six-eight time"). To the right, I'll show you how to count these meters. Of course, if you already know Voggy's Recorder Book, then 4/4- and 3/4 meter are "old friends".

If the word "meter" doesn't mean anything to you, I suggest looking it up in Voggy's Recorder Book (or any other recorder book).

The Notes on Your Recorder

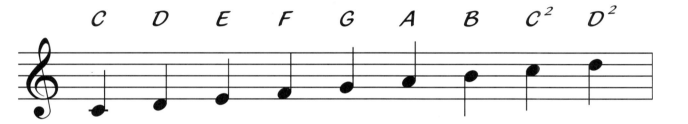

These are the notes you already know if you learned to play with Voggy's Recorder Book. However, for some of the songs in this compendium you'll need two more notes: the note F# (say "F sharp") and the note Bb (say "B flat"). I'll explain them to you on the next page.

Whenever you see the sign ♯ (sharp) in front of the note F, you play an F♯ (F sharp).
On the left, you can see which fingers to use to play the note F♯.

Whenever you see the sign ♭ (flat) in front of the note B, you play a B♭ (B flat).
On the right, you can see which fingers to use to play the note B♭.

The note F#

The note Bb

Key Signatures

If you want every F in a given piece of music to become an F♯, you can indicate this right at the beginning of the staff with a sharp sign on the uppermost line. This means: whenever you encounter an F, play an F♯, thus saving you the trouble of notating a lot of sharps.

You can do the exact same thing with the note B♭:
A flat (♭) notated on the third line of the staff at the beginning of a piece of music means: every B in this piece of music becomes a B♭.
This is called the key signature.

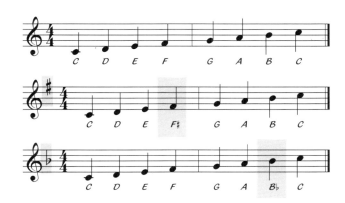

Fingering Chart

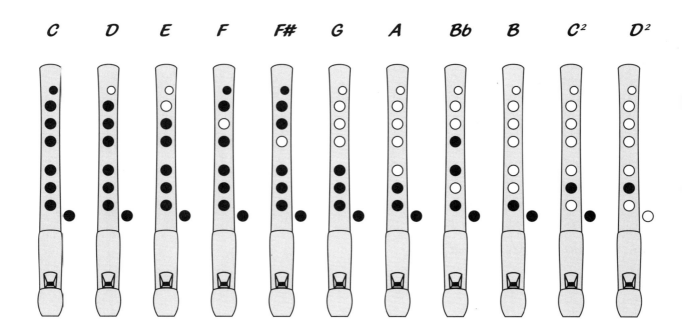

Alphabetical List of Tunes

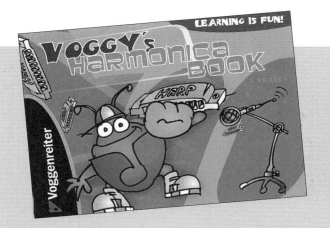

Voggy's Harmonica Book

Little Voggy accompanies your child on the harmonica on his adventure and discovery tours through the fascinating world of music. From the correct way to hold and play it, to learning individual notes, reading music and playing whole tunes. Everything is comprehensively explained in simple terms. For diatonic and Richter harmonicas (Blues harp) in C.

DIN A5 landscape format,
ring binding, 96 pages,
with accompanying CD
ISBN 3-8024-0461-0

VOGGY's Recorder Book

No other instrument compares with the recorder for early musical contact. Accompanied by little Voggy, your child will discover this fascinating world, step by step. From the correct way to hold and play the recorder, to learning individual notes, reading music and playing whole tunes. Everything is comprehensively explained in simple terms.

DIN A5 landscape format,
ring binding, 112 pages
ISBN 3-8024-0464-5

FILET LACE

INTRODUCTION to the LINEN STITCH

MARIE-JO QUINAULT

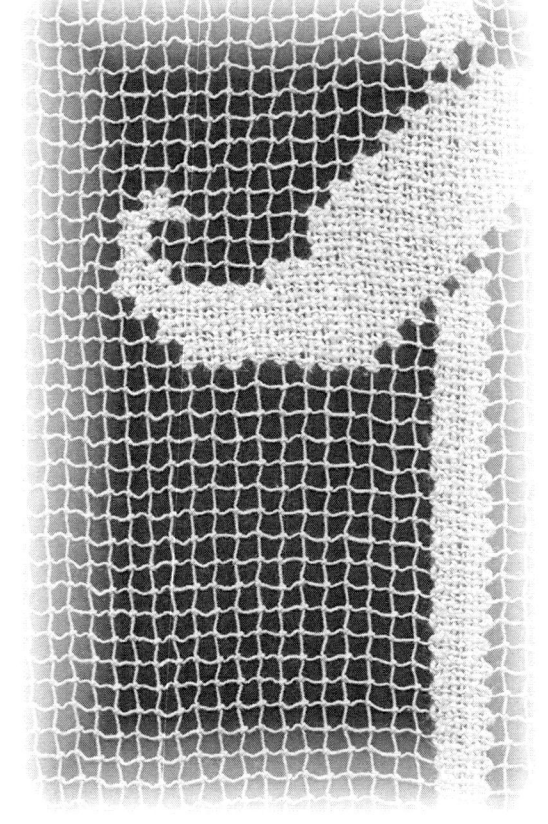

Acknowledgment

*A special thank you to Annette Vickers for her contribution in proof reading ....
Annette, your encouragement and constant support are deeply appreciated.*

Please note ...

*Every effort has been made to ensure that all information in this book
is accurate. However, due to differing conditions, yarns, and individual
needle skills neither the publisher nor the author can be responsible
for any injuries, losses, nor other damages which may result from the
use of the information in this book.*

Cover & back concept, photographs and illustrations, technical edition,
design by Marie-Jo Quinault

All pieces of lace in this book are from Marie-Jo Quinault's personal
collection unless otherwise credited (Page 102-References & Credits).

With love ... to my husband
Michael and to my son Julian for always
believing in me.

Photo No. 1 -- Detail of Linen Stitch on the
"Garden Gate" curtain

A cataloguing record for this book that includes the U.S. Library of Congress Classification number, the Library of Congress Call number
and the Dewey Decimal cataloguing code is available from the National Library of Canada. The complete cataloguing record can be
obtained from the National Library's online database at: www.nlc-bnc.ca/amicus/index-e.html   ISBN: 1-4120-1549-9

TRAFFORD

Suite 6E, 2333 Government St., Victoria, B.C. V8T 4P4, CANADA
Phone	250-383-6864	Toll-free	1-888-232-4444 (Canada & US)
Fax	250-383-6804	E-mail	sales@trafford.com
Web site	www.trafford.com	TRAFFORD PUBLISHING IS A DIVISION OF TRAFFORD HOLDINGS LTD.	
Trafford Catalogue #03-1926		www.trafford.com/robots/03-1926.html	

TABLE OF CONTENTS

FILET LACE · FILET LACE · INTRODUCTION TO THE LINEN STITCH

4

Once upon a time ...
introduction

It all started a long time ago, with fishing net

We do not know when the first filet lace was made, but because fishing nets have been in existence for so long it is believed that Filet Lace is the oldest form of decorative fabric.

The foundation for Filet Lace is an open fabric made of square meshes with a small knot in each corner. It is called the plain filet or Filet net. The *Linen Stitch (Point de Toile)* is the weaving of a thread into the meshes of the filet net to form a cloth. *Filet Lace* (also called *filet work, embroidered netting*) was widely used in the 16th century.

Detail of the Linen Stitch on this Bayeux tapestry panel – on a 3 mm mesh.

Photo 3 – Rare panel of Filet Lace showing scenes based on the Bayeux Tapestry (58" x 14") — Author's collection.
Photo 2 on page 4: Detail of the middle scene

In the beginning, the filet net was knotted by hand using a small shuttle and gauge rod. For a long time, the quantity of netting available was limited to the patience of the artist: knotting a square net is not the most exciting thing to do.

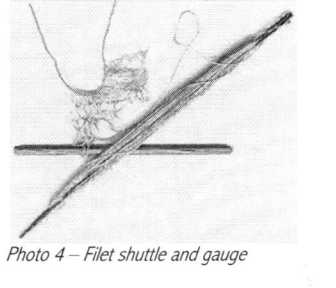

Photo 4 – Filet shuttle and gauge

The first net-making machine, invented in 1812 was commercially used in the 1820s. With the availability of large quantities of knotted fabric, large one-piece curtains and bedspreads could now be created quite quickly.

Photo 5 -- This is the old loom we are using to knot Filet Net 3 for
FILET LACE BY THE SEA.

As it is done today, the fabric was stretched on a frame and the embroidery was done with a long needle using cotton, silk, linen and metallic threads as well as wool.

Filet Lace does not have a unique country of origin: it was made everywhere in the world where fishing net could be found. Over time, lacemakers have developed their own combinations of stitches and threads, putting their own cultures and beliefs into this art form. Depending on this combination Filet Lace has taken different names: *Embroidered filet, Filet-Richelieu, Cut filet lace, Filet- Guipure Lace,* etc.

Scenes consisting of figures and conventional flower designs are mostly executed with the Linen Stitch. Filet-*Guipure Lace* is created with a combination of fancy stitches added to the basic Linen Stitch.

Photo 6 – Peacock from an old German design embroidered in Linen Stitch on
Filet Net 3 by Ruth Youngblood – Detail of her curtain panel

Photo 7 – FILET-GUIPURE on hand made filet net (7" x 7")
Contemporary lace created by Olga Yakunina.

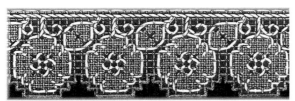

Photo 8 – Example of FILET-RICHELIEU, from Pauline Knight's book.

When the outline of the linen stitch is surrounded by a coarse thread it is called *Filet-Richelieu* or *Cut Filet*.

More modern work is done with different weight and colors of thread to play with different transparencies. Art Nouveau and Art Deco brought their own styles: coarse embroidery, elaborate fringes or tassels and macramé borders are added to the plain filet net to create new designs.

Still available today, you can find these wonderful patterns from as early as the 16th century like the motifs reproduced in this baby bed cover or on the border of the Bayeux Tapestry panel.

Photo 9 – The Unicorn: Pattern from F. Vinciolo 16th century executed by MJ Quinault.

Photo 10– Round collar, contemporary filet lace, Double Linen Stitch on hand made filet net created by Marie-Jo Quinault.

This technique does not require as much patience as you would think: for a project of the same size, bobbin lace or filet crochet would take much longer to realize. With the machine-knotted filet net now available in larger sizes you can complete your curtain panel in a couple of weeks depending on the embroidery on the pattern. You will be enchanted by the ease and speed of accomplishment and the minimum care necessary for your large projects.

Whatever your taste in home decoration, a piece of hand made Filet Lace will never go unnoticed. Medieval "beasties", cascades of vines, cherubs, geometric Art Deco or vestments for Church, your project made with Filet Net 3 and Filet Net 5 merits a place in your daily modern life.

Photo 11 – Antique Baby bed cover 42"x42": Filet Lace and Cutwork embroidery. Author's collection.

MATERIALS and ACCESSORIES
To start the Embroidery on Knotted Net - Filet Lace

THE TRADITIONAL FILET NET - This fabric has been used for centuries as the foundation for the technique of Filet Lace. It is a fine square knotted net (an individual fisherman's knot in each corner of the mesh) made of soft 100% cotton thread. These two nets are mechanically made on an old loom as it was done in the 19e century.

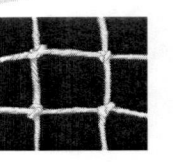

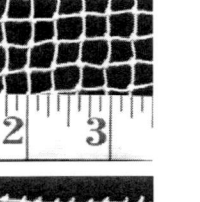

FILET NET No. 3 -- 3 meshes per inch; this size mesh is suggested for curtain panels and other large pieces. It is the perfect size mesh for learning. With this mesh, use thread DMC Coton Perlé No. 3 or the equivalent in size for a light lace; for a heavy lace, use an 8-ply thread.

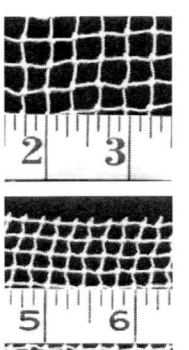

FILET NET No. 5 -- 5 meshes per inch; this size mesh is recommended for tapestry, pillows, clothing, and most projects. In fact, your creativity will dictate your choice of mesh size. With this mesh, use the thread DMC Coton Perlé No. 5 or the equivalent in size.

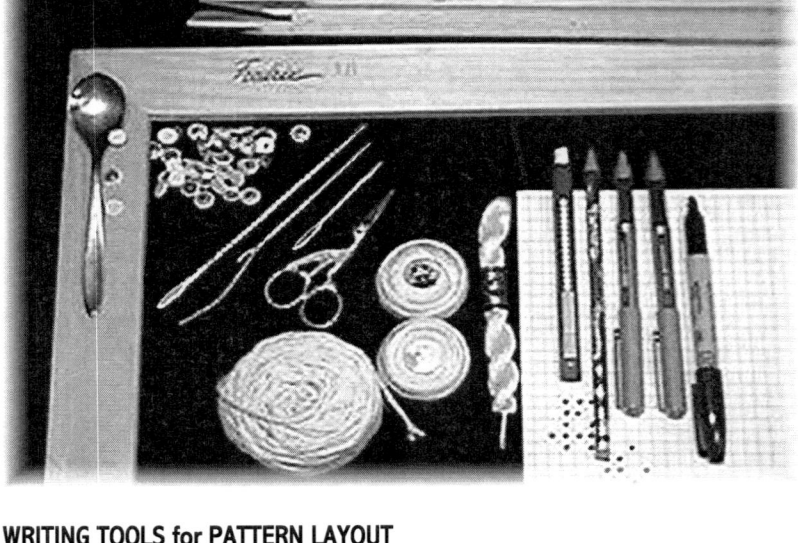

WRITING TOOLS for PATTERN LAYOUT
Graph paper, 4 or 5 squares per inch (or per 2.5 cm)
A soft pencil HB and/or B
A comfortable eraser, Scotch tape,
A black "Sharpie" marker (fine point) to mark the dots
A gel ink pen to draw the path on the pattern (red, pink or light color)

Small Scissors

A LONG NEEDLE -- This is a strong 6" long (15.5 cm) weaving needle with a dull triangular tip. This is the perfect needle to speed up weaving on large pieces of Filet Net 3.
The alternative is a tatting needle 5" long (12.5 cm).

THE BALLPOINT NEEDLE -- This must-have needle is 3.5" long (9 cm). It is fine, has a long eye and a small ball at the tip. This needle makes it easier to weave on filet net and tulle; it grasps the thread and does not let go easily.
The alternative is a size 13 tapestry needle.

FRAME & THUMBTACKS -- 18"x 24" (46cmx60cm)
This frame is made of "Fredrix" stretcher bars found in the Oil Painting department of craft stores. They are sold in different lengths so you can build a frame the size you need for your different projects. The alternative is to make your own frame or to use a hoop as large as possible between 24" to 36" diameter (approx. 60 to 90 cm). To fix the filet net on the frame, use small thumbtacks from the hardware store and a spoon to push and pull.

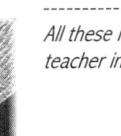

All these items are available in a store near you, through the teacher in your area, at our Studio or Online.

Visit our web page for more information
FILET LACE BY THE SEA
www.filetlace.net

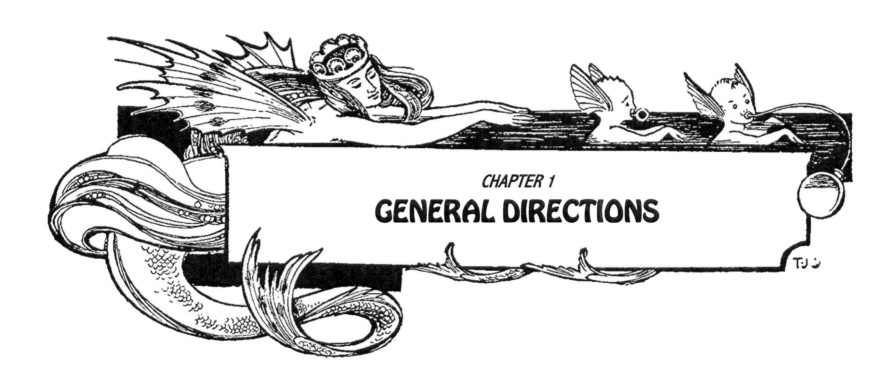

CHAPTER 1

GENERAL DIRECTIONS

HOW TO USE THIS METHOD

There are several ways to draw the path of the Linen Stitch. They are all good if they reach the goal: fill the dotted meshes, avoid the empty ones, and achieve a perfect weaving without excess of thread.

My concept is just one method that allows you to learn the technique quickly so you can realize projects as large as you want, in a short of time.

The master key of this concept is to know how to work the path of the needle on paper first. The work on filet net becomes simpler as you follow the path like a map.

To learn this technique, the following steps are recommended:

- Reproduce all the exercises and patterns on your ¼" grid paper. Do not photocopy as you must learn to reproduce the patterns accurately.

- Take each level one at a time. Practice the exercises of each level on paper first until you can draw the paths of all the patterns and exercises without referring to the book.

- Then return to the beginning of the same chapter and learn how to do the embroidery on filet net.

- Always keep your paperwork clean and precise.

- Attain the goals of each level before starting the next one. Proceed slowly. When in doubt, go back and redo earlier exercises, re-reading the instructions out loud, and

studying the illustrations and photos of the step-by-step section. With your pencil trace over the paths already done and understand the rules and directions.

- Always work with the description of the 4 keys in front of you and repeat them out loud. Talk to yourself; describe each of your actions: *"…changing direction … always do the returns of… horizontal row from right to left, hidden stitch"*, etc.

- Do the exercises on paper every day for a few weeks to ensure your progress, especially while learning Chapter 5. And even if you feel you do not understand or think you are not making progress, continue.

Do not compare with other techniques while learning this method. This concept being different, it could be confusing and slow down your learning.

BE PERSISTENT, BE PATIENT, AND DO NOT GIVE UP: KNOWLEDGE IS IN YOUR HANDS!

It takes concentration, tenacity and daily exercises to learn this needle art technique. It is normal to feel overwhelmed at Level 3. Be persistent, take a break and return later with a rested mind: the technique will suddenly come to you. You are going to be a winner!

So open the door and do not be intimidated.

A COMFORTABLE SET-UP

Take the time to organize a comfortable environment. Choose a quiet place to achieve the level of concentration required for the early learning; once learned you will even be able to follow a movie while making Filet Lace.

STABILIZE THE FRAME
Because installing the filet net on the frame is not the most enjoyable part of the embroidery, it is recommended you use a wood frame (or a large hoop) the size of the lace to avoid having to move the net.

The frame should not move; use the edge of a table and place the bottom of the frame on your lap. There are also several commercial universal craft stands you could use to hold small frames and hoops (picture on the right).

You can build your own frame. Mine, built of stretcher bars, is affordable and practical; it is attached to a movable floor partition using a system of chains and clips on the front. I can quickly change the height and position of small to very large sized frames. The bottom of the frame is either on my lap or remains vertical. I use a chair and sometimes sit on a foot stool, to be at the proper height on the lower working surface. As much as possible, I keep my arms at waist level and my back straight.

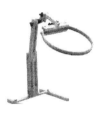

A TABLE AT YOUR SIDE
Have a table at your right on which to place your pattern, thread and tools (opposite side for left-handers).

APPROPRIATE LIGHTING
Good lighting is important as this fabric is made up of holes. A contrasting fabric installed on the back of your frame will minimize eye strain; attach the fabric to the top back and place the bottom on your lap (do not attach the lower part as you need to access the back of your work).

Natural daylight is still the best light and comfortable surroundings make the embroidery pleasant and relaxing.

THE EMBROIDERY FRAME

This soft 100% cotton knotted fabric needs to be stabilized in order to work on it.

Metal frames or specialized stretchers for filet lace are used for smaller projects or on a very fine filet net.

Hoops are also used if the motif of your project does not require you to go in to the corners (waste of material).

However, when doing a very large project using Filet Net 3 and Filet Net 5, the wood stretcher bars & thumbtacks are much quicker to install, more practical for storage and by any means, less expensive. After all, the interesting part is to do the embroidery!

STRETCH THE FILET NET ON THE FRAME

Assemble the stretcher bars to form the frame size that will fit your design. If your project is too large for the frame (as for a larger curtain) the filet net would need to be repositioned to complete the pattern. The stretcher bars, available in the Oil Painting department of craft stores, are available to a length of 60 inches (152 cm).

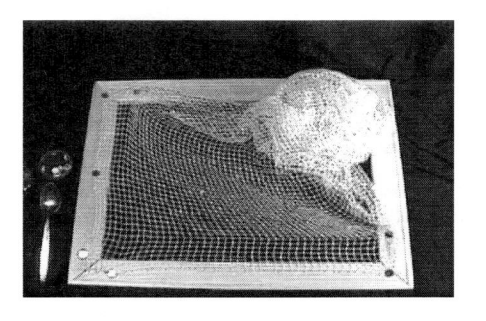

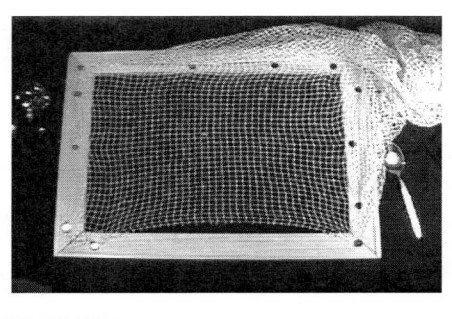

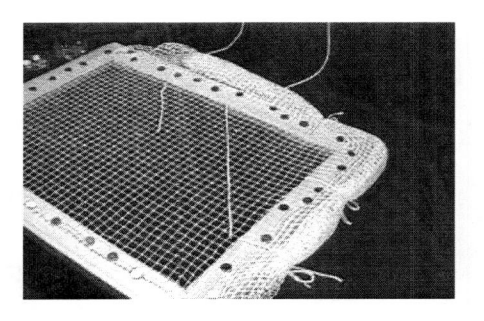

START ON THE LOWER LEFT CORNER

Start by applying one thumbtack at the lower left corner. Stretch the net and put another thumbtack at the upper left corner keeping the filet net mesh aligned with the stretcher bar.
Repeat for the lower right corner.
Next, apply a thumbtack in the middle or each side.
Stretch taut and square the netting to the upper right corner of the stretcher bars.
Secure with thumbtacks at every inch.

SQUARE AND TIGHT

Do not be afraid to really stretch Filet Net 3 or Filet Net 5 square on the frame. The net should be almost as tight as the strings on a tennis racquet. *(But be gentle when using the finer thread filet net).*

You can use a pusher or the back of a spoon to push or pull the thumbtacks.

If the filet net becomes loose while doing the embroidery, retighten it to make it taut. It is easier to work on a tight net.

ATTACH THE LEFTOVER FILET NET OUT OF THE WAY

Tightly roll the leftover filet net and attach it with strings to the frame. Push the roll to the back of the frame, and move the ties out of the way.

Your frame is now ready to use.

TYING THE KNOTS

These simple knots are very strong and easy for the beginner. There are other specialized knots that can be used to reach the same goal.

THE TEMPORARY KNOT

Use the Temporary knot to determine the mesh where your pattern will begin.
Place this knot on the lowest horizontal thread of the selected mesh.
Count twice to be sure of your starting point on the filet net or the shape will be off center.

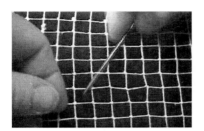

As shown, pass the needle underneath the bottom thread of the chosen filet mesh.

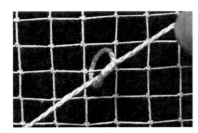

Make a simple knot leaving 4" to 6" of thread. Place the knot on the left side.

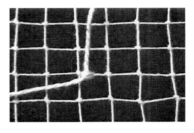

Do not tighten too much. It must be untied later. Push the end of the thread to the back

If the thread interferes with your work, twist it around the meshes or squeeze it under a thumbtack.

THE PERMANENT KNOT

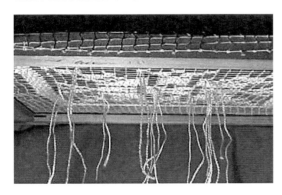

Your goal is to avoid making too many knots at the back of your work. To accomplish this, use long lengths of thread: 5 or 6 yards, sometime longer.

When this length of thread is used up, start a new length at the same place, keeping all the threads at the back of the work. Then turn your frame and make all the Permanent knots.

Knots can interfere with the transparency of the lace. In general, we do not reweave to hide knots: this adds more thickness to the mesh. When well done, the Permanent knots will pass the washing machine test and fall into place after several washings.

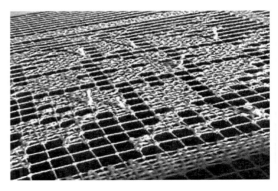

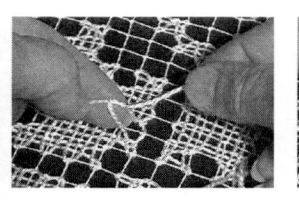  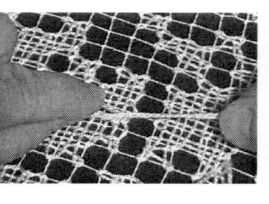 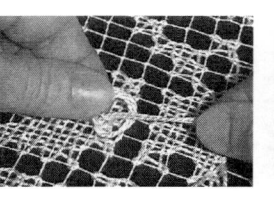 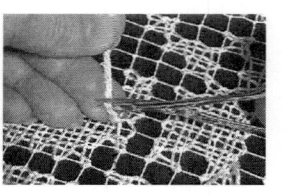

Turn the frame to the wrong side. Place the thread ends to be knotted over a filet net thread.	Make a simple knot. Position the knot close to the work, without pulling so as not to deform the row.	Over it, make a double knot (surgeons knot) passing twice in the loop. Then tighten the knot over the first one.	Over these 2 knots, make another simple knot and tighten it well.	Fold the two threads together on your finger and make a knot. Push both threads together, very close to the others and tighten it as much as possible.	Cut the threads, leaving ¼" of thread after the knot. This thread will shrink when washed.

THE FINISHING KNOT

The Finishing knot is a Permanent knot done with the beginning thread (the Temporary knot) and the ending thread. This knot is generally located at the edge of the pattern. Special care should be taken to ensure that the knot will not be seen at the edge. It should disappear at the time of washing and blocking.

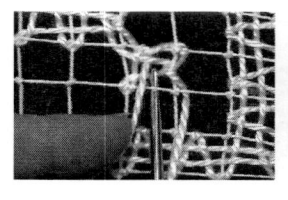  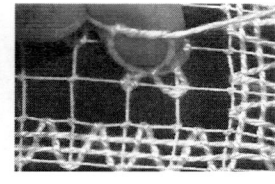 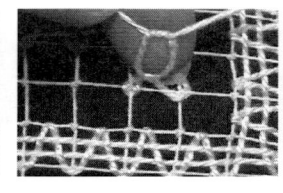  

Undo the Temporary knot and hold it with the left hand. With the needle reweave to reach the middle of the mesh; a knot made too close to the edge of the mesh will show.	Make a simple knot. Position the knot close to the work without pulling, so as to not deform the row.	Make a double knot over it and tighten.	Over these 2 knots, make another single knot and tighten it well.	Fold the two threads together on your finger and make a knot. Push it very close to the others and tighten it as much as possible.	Cut the threads, leaving ¼" of thread after the knot. The thread will shrink when washed.

Photo No. 12 – Detail in the Bayeux tapestry border

THE CHOICE OF THREADS

A variety of threads can be used with Filet Lace: cotton, linen, silk, wool, or metallic.
The resulting thickness of the lace depends on the size of thread and the stitch used.

Certain laces are made with a very thick cotton thread as for curtains (cotton mesh);
others are very light (equivalent to DMC Coton Perlé No. 8, 12) when used with the Double Linen Stitch.
The best way to decide which is appropriate for your project is to work a sample first;
measure it, wash & bleach; dry and then measure it again.
See if this is the desired result.

In general, if you use DMC Coton Perlé 3 or the equivalent with Filet Net 3 and DMC Coton perlé 5
or the equivalent with Filet Net 5, you should have as a result a beautiful project.

COTTON SHRINKS AND IT IS A GOOD THING

Because filet net is made of 100% cotton, shrinkage should be calculated when starting a project.
Depending on the project and on the chosen thread, calculate shrinkage between 10% and 20%.

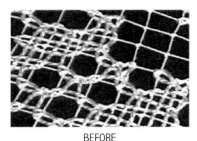

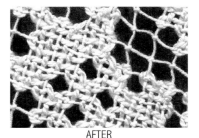

BEFORE

Linen Stitch on Filet Net 3 with a DMC Coton Perlé No. 3
still on the frame.

AFTER

The same part of the lace after washing, bleaching &
drying. With time, cotton will fluff and fill the spaces.

WHITE LACE

Use bleach as directed to obtain a white lace. The use of too much bleach will weaken the fibers.
The filet net is made with 100% cotton and will naturally become whiter after years of use.
Test a sample before doing your embroidery; be sure the thread used for your project can also be bleached.

FINISHING THE LACE

Finishing a piece of lace includes making an edge by adding a needle or crocheted row, another kind of small lace or very large lace, a fringe or pompons. The work can be extensive, depending on your choice. The Buttonhole Stitch is the traditional and simple way to finish the edge of a Filet Lace.

BOTTONHOLE STITCH BORDER

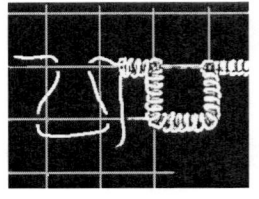
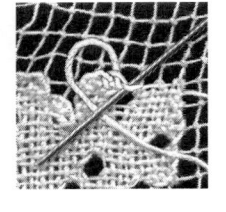

It is easier to make this stitch when the filet is still on the frame.

The number of stitches in each mesh depends on the size of the thread. Using the same thread as the embroidery (here DMC Coton Perlé 5 on Filet Net 5), make 3 Buttonhole stitches per mesh; more if the thread is smaller. Do not make too many stitches as it will tighten and warp after washing.

Hide the knot and threads at the edge of the lace, in the Buttonhole Stitch, not in the weaving.

You can add a thread to stabilize the edge. Pass a thread on the edge of the motif as shown in the photograph, and then make the Buttonhole Stitch.

Once the edge is completed, cut the filet net leaving ¼" of net thread from the Filet Knot as shown in the photograph.

CROCHET BORDER

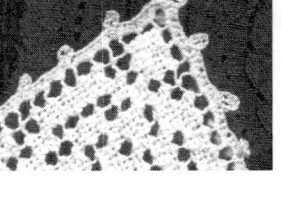
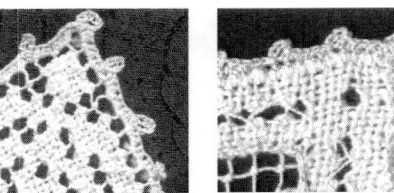
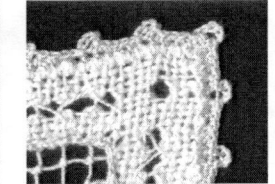

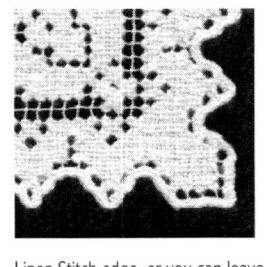

Cut the filet net first, leaving ¼", and do not stretch the filet as the knots in each corners are now vulnerable.

Use a finer thread: crochet stitches double the weight. Verify as you proceed to be sure the edge does not have too many stitches to avoid buckling.

You can do the border directly on the Linen Stitch edge, or you can leave one mesh-space between the motif and the border to create another design.

ADD A TRIM TO THE BORDER

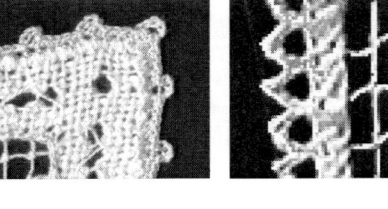
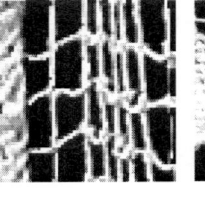
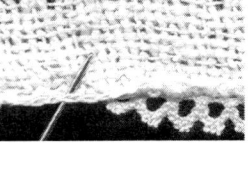

You may want to add a cotton lace. It can be a tiny Cluny lace like this one (3/8" or 1cm) or a very large cut work lace (Richelieu embroidery). To be well-balanced the addition must be of a heavier texture.

Add fringe, pompons, or macramé made with the same weight thread.

The Cluny lace is attached to the edge with a row of crochet, using a smaller weight thread than used for the embroidery. Be careful not to stretch the edge of the filet net while adding the crochet / Cluny lace. Or make a Buttonhole Stitch to attach the lace to the filet lace.

CURTAIN or TAPESTRY

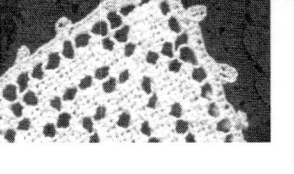

You can use the designer way to make the head of a curtain; here are simple ways to hang filet lace curtains.

For example here, finish the edge with a crochet row on the edge of the Linen Stitch and use clip rings to hang the piece. Or build a pocket at the head: fold between 8" to 10" (20 to 25 cm), enough for the pole to pass through loosely; attach the two parts together with a Buttonhole Stitch using a needle or a row of crochet.

CARING FOR YOUR FILET LACE
Made with Filet Net 3 and Filet Net 5

HAND WASH

Soak and hand wash small pieces. Rinse very well.
Shape and dry flat after the first few washes: block and iron your first piece while still damp; later this step may become unnecessary. Use a pressing cloth and the proper heat setting to avoid burning the fibers. Try not to snag the meshes with the iron.

USING THE WASHING MACHINE

For larger pieces and curtains made with washable thread on Filet Net 3 and Filet Net 5, fill the washing machine tub and soak the lace. Stir once in a while or use the "Hand-wash" cycle only if you have made strong knots. Then use the spinning cycle to extract the water. Repeat to rinse completely.

For pieces with delicate / raised embroidery and for the finer filet net, wash in a pillow case (a body pillow case works well for very large pieces) or use special mesh bags.

Use the Spin cycle and double rinse. Re-hang straight on the pole without folds. Reshape/stretch with your hands if necessary.

Use fabric softener in the rinse cycle to facilitate untangling the fringe.

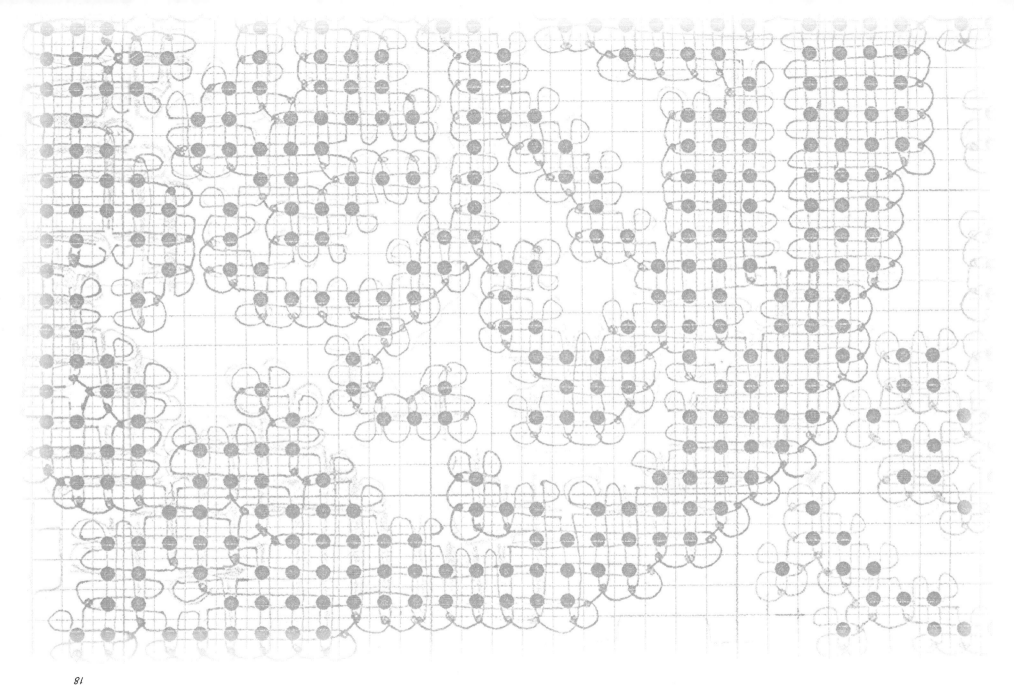

CHAPTER 2

THE PATTERN

MAKE YOUR OWN PATTERN

MAKE THE DOTS

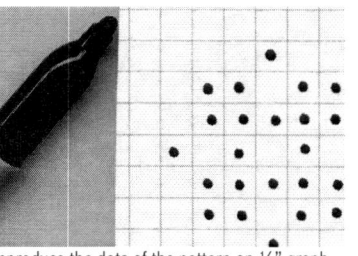

Reproduce the dots of the pattern on ¼" graph paper (no smaller) using the Sharpie permanent marker. Place each dot exactly in the middle of the square

If the marker is new, press the tip vertically on paper until it makes a nice big round dot after just one push.

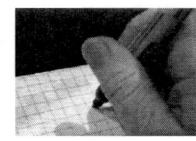

DRAW THE PATH

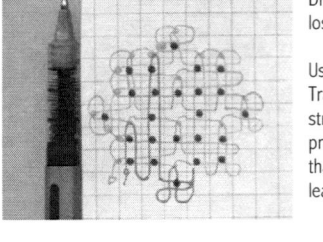

Draw the path with a pencil first. If you become lost, erase the whole thing and start over.

Use extra care when drawing the lines and loops: Trace the lines on each side of the dots, as straight as possible, and the loops in the right proportions. Do not make lines bigger or smaller than indicated; a messy drawing will slow you in learning the technique.

Look at section "Calligraphy for the Linen Stitch" to learn how to draw the perfect path.

When the path is completed, pass over the pencil marks with a pink ink pen (or light blue or light green). Then erase the pencil marks to reveal a perfect filet lace pattern ready to begin. A good drawing is easy to read and it will speed up the work on the filet net.

Date your pattern and write the reference of its origin, with the author's name. Keep your patterns: you may want to use a part of this drawing for a future project.

FOLLOW YOUR PATTERN

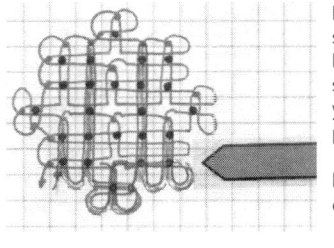

Place your pattern flat on the side table. With a pencil (soft lead B to B4) pass over a small section of the path. Then with your needle, reproduce this path with thread on the filet net.

Return to your pattern, pass over another small section

and then repeat it on the filet net. Start with a small section at a time. With practice you will be able to remember a larger section as you will be gaining speed and confidence.

When you stop in the middle of your work, place a marker (here a "Post-it" arrow) to retrieve your place as shown on the picture. It is a good idea to use it when you have to remember many entrances.

When you have finished your lace, erase the pencil marks on your pattern, roll or fold it and keep it for future use.

ENLARGE YOUR GRAPH PAPER

A larger pad of ¼" graph paper (17" x 22") can be found on the market, but if it is not large enough, you need to assemble sheets together before making the dots. The following is a nice clean way to do it:

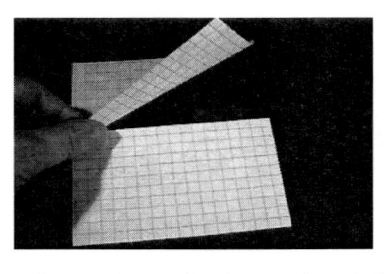

Cut one top sheet very close to a line. Apply scotch tape to the back of the lower sheet to temporarily hold them together while adjusting. Carefully overlap the squares of the top sheet to the second sheet. Turn both sheets over and tape along the seam. This is the back of the pattern.

To secure the front, glue the entire length of the edge of the paper (use the Double Stick Adhesive-permanent glue). Press the seam well for a very flat surface. This will be the front of your pattern, without tape, glue or lumps that could interfere with the ink while drawing your pattern.

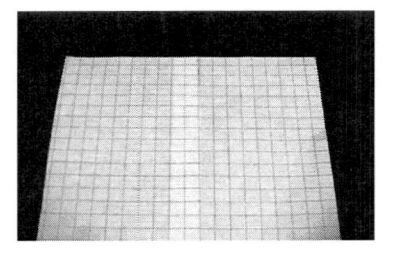

The enlarged sheet will have a continuous grid with no tape on the front to interfere with the drawing or the ink.

CALLIGRAPHY OF THE LINEN STITCH

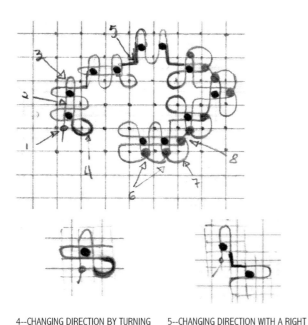

1--The TEMPORARY KNOT is depicted by a small circle with a tail at the bottom of the starting mesh

2--The STRAIGHT LINES are parallel and close to the dot. This is the part of the thread weaving into the mesh.

3--THE LOOP is a small curve and passes slightly over the line.

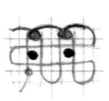

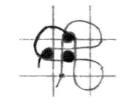

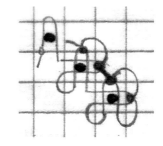

4--CHANGING DIRECTION BY TURNING AROUND THE FILET KNOT should be a generous turn around the filet knot. Over-exaggerating the movement is better than making it too small. This is done in all four directions.

5--CHANGING DIRECTION WITH A RIGHT ANGLE should be made as a corner, with a very nice right angle. This is done in all four directions.

6--The HIDDEN STITCH is a big colored dot at the top of the loop. It fills the whole space, touching the line of the filet net. HIDDEN STITCHES IN A ROW are represented by large dots linked by scallops that meet.

7--HIDDEN STITCH -TURNING AROUND THE FILET KNOT: This is a big dot on the loop which combines with a large turn around the filet knot as shown in 4.

8--HIDDEN STITCH ON THE INSIDE: Not a scallop or curved line: it is a straight direct line going from one loop to another.

POOR DRAWINGS
A bad drawing (below) can confuse and make you lost!

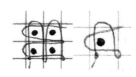

Draw lines parallel and straight close to the dots. These changes of direction around the knot of the filet net are too skimpy.

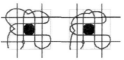

In this illustration, Hidden Stitches are missing at the tip of the loop. The change of direction is too short around the filet knot corner, between the two Hidden stitches.

DO YOU HAVE TROUBLE WITH THE PROPORTIONS?

Hi! I'm Mermie!

Try using this template. Reproduce these dotted lines on your graph paper and practice the proportions

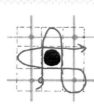

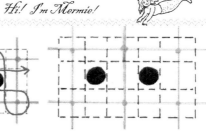

Welcome to my world!

Being lost in the network of mangroves without a map or tools can be pretty scary! Mapping the trip to know where you are going before leaving ensures a nice and smooth journey. In filet lace we call it making the "path".

The "path" on paper is the navigation of your needle before you start the embroidery on the filet net. My 4 keys will help you reach all the dots and avoid the empty ones.

Practice knowing how to recognize each situation and you will be able to realize very large and intricate designs without difficulty.

Carefully follow the directions: I'll be swimming around to help you with little hints.

Hi!

I'm Mermie

Mermie's 4 keys
to unlock the secrets of the
Linen Stitch

Key No. 1
Always start on the left side, at the lowest row of the pattern, vertically, going up.

Key No. 2
Always complete the parallel *returns* right away, on all your horizontal / vertical rows.

Key No. 3
Use the Hidden Stitch to hide the thread and reach other groups of meshes on the pattern,

Key No. 4
This key is the exception to Key No. 2
It is used ONLY if you are starting a HORIZONTAL-ROW-GOING-FROM-RIGHT-TO-LEFT, and when you MEET-A-POOL-SITUATION. Use the Hidden Stitch (or a vertical row going down) to bypass the empty mesh. Do not immediately complete the *return* on the row: continue to the left as far as possible as you meet new "Pool situations". When there are no more "Pool situations" on the left, turn and complete all the *returns* using the vertical row (going up) to bypass the empty mesh.

If it is not a "Pool Situation", it is a "Bay Situation"; use Key No. 2 and Key No. 3

Marie-Jo QUINAULT

Photo 13 – Valance for a canopy bed

CHAPTER 3
LEVEL 1 – THE LINEN STITCH

GOALS for LEVEL 1

~ Know how to use Keys No. 1 and No. 2 ~
~ Navigate the Path with the "Change of Direction" ~
~ Achieve a perfect weaving without mistakes ~
~ Begin the pattern on the proper mesh ~
~ Know the "Temporary knot" and the "Permanent knot" ~

Reach these goals before starting Level 2

BASICS OF THE LINEN STITCH

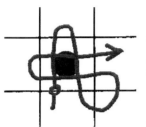

PATTERN ON PAPER

One dot on the pattern is made up of two vertical and two horizontal lines.

Within these two vertical lines there is the "Go" and the "Return". There is also a "Go" and a "Return" within the horizontal lines.

Knowing how to draw the "Path" is crucial to achieving larger patterns. The "Path" is the navigation of your needle through the maze of all the dots on your design.

A well-drawn pattern will hasten the learning process. (Refer also to the Calligraphy of the Linen Stitch in Chapter 2). Reproduce this template to learn the proportion of those lines, loops and turns. When you have finished drawing your path in pencil, trace over it with your gel pen, then erase the pencil lines to reveal a complete pattern.

1. THE PATTERN
Reproduce the single dot on your ¼" graph paper using the black marker.
Hold the marker perpendicular and press firmly once to the center of the square, to produce a large round dot. If the dot is too small, press the marker several times on a piece of waste paper to gently flatten the tip.

2. THE TEMPORARY KNOT
This marks the beginning of this path. With your pencil, draw a small circle on the line at the base of the square (the square represents the mesh on the filet net), and add a small line under the circle. There can be several starting points on a pattern.

3. THE FIRST PART OF THE VERTICAL ROW
Draw a vertical line going upward. The line should touch the black dot on its left and not touch the line of the graph paper. Pass slightly above the upper line.
This is the first part of the vertical row.

4. THE RETURN ON THE VERTICAL ROW
Form a small loop at the top and draw a parallel line going down, touching the right side of the black dot, and passing the horizontal line slightly on the graph paper.
This is the second part of the vertical row.

5. CHANGE DIRECTION BY TURNING AROUND THE SMALL KNOT OF THE FILET NET
This allows you to do the horizontal row right away. Draw a large circle around the small knot of the filet net (the corner of the graph paper square). Over-exaggerating the movement is better than making it too small.

6. THE FIRST PART OF THE HORIZONTAL ROW
Draw a horizontal line from right to left touching the bottom of the black dot and slightly passing to the left of the vertical line.

7. DRAW THE LOOP
The loop should not extend too much outside of the square (with the dot).
No oversized loop is allowed as it could interfere with another part on the pattern. Follow the template.

Take extra care in drawing your lines and curves. The learning process will be easier if the drawing of your paths is clean and well done.

8. THE RETURN ON THE HORIZONTAL ROW
From the left side, turn to form a small loop. Draw the parallel line going from left to right touching the top of the black dot and passing the vertical line on the graph paper. Finish with an arrow marking the end of this path.

LET'S BE VERY ACCURATE
a) This is the beginning of a row: A row starts at this point and not before.
b) This is the end of a row. The return row is completed only when the pencil drawing the line passes the junction "b".

Be sure to always extend your line beyond this junction before making a decision on looking for the next direction.

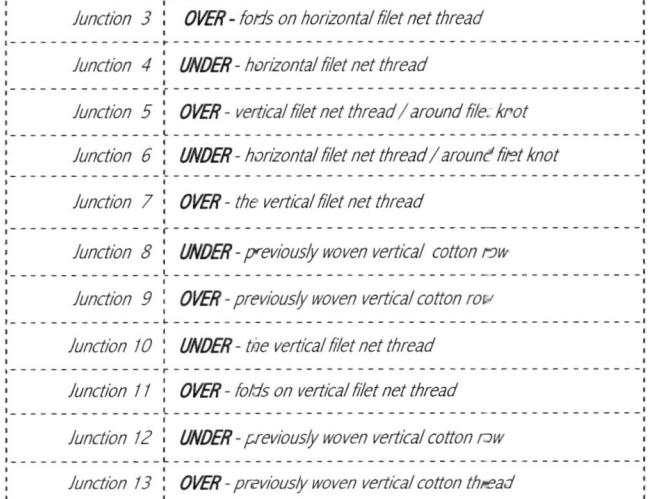

EMBROIDERY ON THE FILET NET

The LINEN STITCH is one of the basic stitches traditionally used for filet lace. It is produced by weaving in and out onto the meshes of the filet net, horizontally and vertically to create a linen fabric.

The junction (with the numbers) occurs when your needle is crossing a thread (the filet net thread or a thread that you have previously woven).

This continuous action of alternating (*Over-Under*) on every single junction in all directions will insure a perfect Linen Stitch. Falling out of this sequence will produce an error in the weaving and the rest of your work will not coincide.

To better understand the weaving order, follow the numbered photograph on the left and the table on the right, speaking out loud at each crossing point, starting with junction 1 (Temporary Knot).

Did you notice these? Junctions 2 & 3 have the same support filet thread. The same situation applies with junctions 10 & 11. Then at junctions 4, 5, 6 & 7: junction 4 is the exit of the vertical row while 7 is the entrance for the horizontal row. On junctions 5 & 6 the thread is changing direction around the small knot of the filet net. Note the consistency of the weaving on junctions 4, 5, 6 and 7 (*Under-Over-Under-Over*).

It is basically simple: always alternate the *"Under"*, *"Over"* motions, counting-every-single-thread-your-needle-meets (junction), whatever the direction.

FOLLOWING THE PATTERN STEP-BY-STEP

- Place your own pattern flat on the table and install the filet net on your embroidery frame (Refer to Chapter 1).
- Prepare a needle with one yard of cotton thread (here we are using DMC Coton Perlé No. 3 on Filet Net No. 3)
- Reproduce the path of your pattern on the filet net.

TABLE - FOLLOW THE JUNCTIONS OF THIS PATH

This table is the written actions of this One-mesh pattern. It shows you the continuity in those *"Under"* & *"Over"* motions.

Junction 1	Temporary knot (considered **Over**)
Junction 2	**UNDER** - horizontal filet net thread
Junction 3	**OVER** - folds on horizontal filet net thread
Junction 4	**UNDER** - horizontal filet net thread
Junction 5	**OVER** - vertical filet net thread / around filet knot
Junction 6	**UNDER** - horizontal filet net thread / around filet knot
Junction 7	**OVER** - the vertical filet net thread
Junction 8	**UNDER** - previously woven vertical cotton row
Junction 9	**OVER** - previously woven vertical cotton row
Junction 10	**UNDER** - the vertical filet net thread
Junction 11	**OVER** - folds on vertical filet net thread
Junction 12	**UNDER** - previously woven vertical cotton row
Junction 13	**OVER** - previously woven vertical cotton thread
Junction 14	**UNDER** - the vertical filet net thread to exit

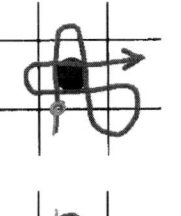

1. THE TEMPORARY KNOT

Following on the pattern: with your pencil, retrace the section of the Temporary knot as shown on the drawing on your left.
Now, on the filet net, tie the Temporary knot. This is Junction 1 and it is considered an *Over* motion.
The temporary knot attaches the thread at the right place, thus avoiding the shifting of the pattern on the netting.

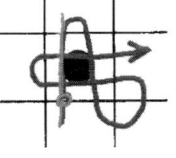

2. START THE VERTICAL ROW

On the pattern: with your pencil, retrace the section of your path from junction 1 to junction 2.
Now, on the filet net, with the needle in your right hand, pass the needle *under* junction 2.
Pull the thread.

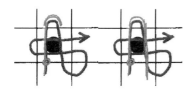

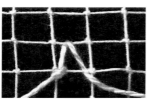

3. COMPLETE THE RETURN ON THIS VERTICAL ROW

On the pattern: with your pencil, retrace the path going from junction 3 to junction 4.
Repeat the same action on the filet net. Junctions 2 and 3 are using the same filet net thread but it does not matter: these are two separate steps: the thread passes *UNDER* junction 2 and folds *OVER* junction 3.
Pass *Over* junction 4 and pull the thread.
You have now completed the vertical row.

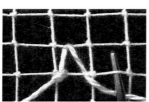

4. CHANGING DIRECTION BY TURNING AROUND THE SMALL KNOT OF THE FILET NET

Retrace the next step on your pattern.
Then, holding the needle in your left hand, pass *over* junction 5 and *under* junction 6.
Pull the thread.
You are now ready to start the horizontal row.

5. START THE HORIZONTAL ROW

The horizontal row has more junctions because of the vertical row you have just done and all the threads must be counted as a single step.
With your needle horizontally over junction 7, weave the whole sequence together, which makes:

- *OVER* filet net thread junction 7,
- *UNDER* previously woven thread junction 8
- *OVER* previously woven cotton thread junction 9
- *UNDER* the filet net thread at junction 10

Pull the needle with your left hand.

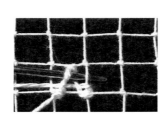

6. COMPLETE THE RETURN OF THE HORIZONTAL ROW

With your needle in your left hand weave the following:
Over, Under, Over, Under
and pull the needle with your right hand.

Here is the detail:

- Folding *OVER* at junction 11
- *UNDER* junction 12 (your vertical row)
- *OVER* junction 13 (your vertical row)
- *UNDER* junction 14 (the filet net thread)
-

The one-mesh pattern is now complete and perfectly woven.

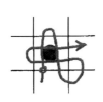

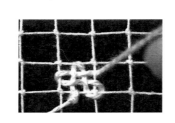

ADJUST THE TENSION

The example in the photograph is woven loosely to show the details of the *under* and *over* motions. However, as your netting is as tight as tennis racquet cords, the thread should be pulled tightly each time, but should not deform the shape of the mesh. It is easy to achieve when your filet net is well stretched.

A VERTICAL ROW

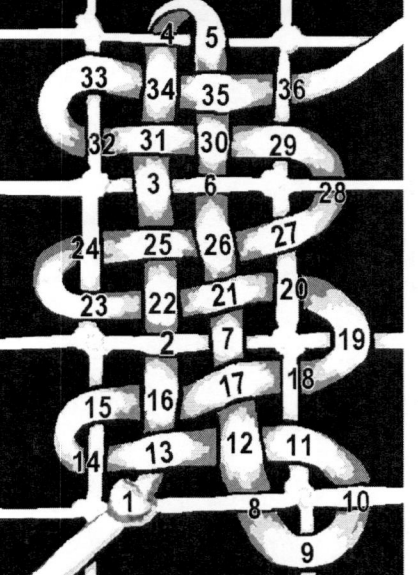

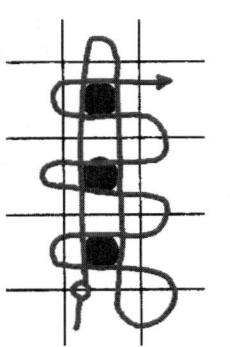

Key No. 1:
Start on the left side, at the lowest row of the pattern, vertically, going up.

Key No. 2:
Always complete the parallel Returns on all your rows (vertical and horizontal)

PATTERN ON PAPER

It is also "a row" when there is more than one dot in the same direction. When there is a row, draw the line to complete the whole row: do not do one dot at a time, do not stop in the middle of the row and always complete the full Return on the row... never stop before the row is completed.

Reproduce this pattern on your ¼" graph paper and draw this path using a pencil.

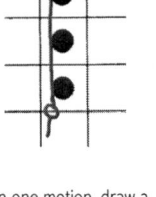
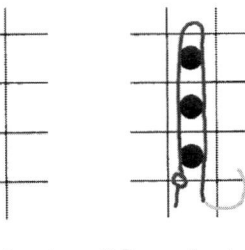
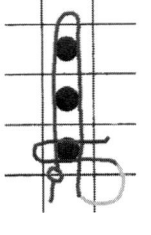
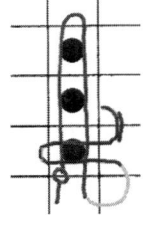
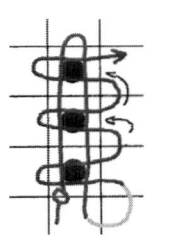

1. This pattern is one vertical row. There are 3 consecutive dots in this row.

2. Start with a small circle on the bottom horizontal of the chosen mesh. This is to show the Temporary knot, the starting point of your path on the paper.

3. In one motion, draw a vertical line going up. (Read Key No. 1)

4. To complete the *return* on the vertical row, form a loop slightly over the line and draw a vertical line downward. (Read Key No. 2)

5. Because there is no vertical row on the right, it is now time to *change direction*, with a large motion, turn the corner (turn around the Filet knot).

6. Draw the first of the 3 consecutive horizontal rows, going to the left from the loop and complete the parallel *return* on this row. (Read Key No. 2)

7. To reach the next horizontal row, turn the corner on the outside horizontal thread (the double line); draw a large scallop.

8. Repeat to complete the 2 remaining horizontal rows and finish with a small arrow to show the end of this path.

EMBROIDERY ON THE FILET NET

Mark your pattern with a pencil, a little section at a time, as you do the embroidery on the filet net.

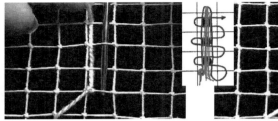
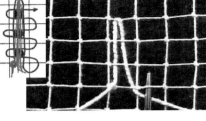

1. Start with a temporary knot at the bottom of the starting mesh (This is junction 1 *over*).

2. Key No. 1: Always start vertically, going up. Always start weaving *under* (junction No. 2) with your needle In the right hand. Pull the thread with the left hand.

3. Complete the parallel *return* on the row (Key No. 2) with your needle in the right hand.
Under junction 4; junction 5 folds *over* the same thread of the filet net.

4. *Change direction* by turning your needle around the small knot of the filet net: Junction 9 *over* and junction 10 *under*.

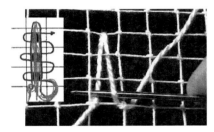
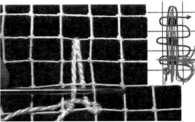
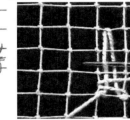
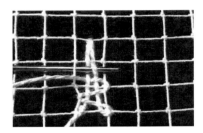

5. Start the horizontal row going left.
The *under / over* rule applies to all junctions found on the way (11-12-13-14).

6. Key No. 2 —Complete the *return* on your horizontal row. Junctions 15-16-17-18. The needle is now in your left hand.

7. There are 3 horizontal meshes to complete on this pattern; to reach the second mesh, pass *over* junction 19 and then do the horizontal row (20-21-22-23).

8. Do the *return* on this horizontal row. Junctions 24-25-26-27. The second mesh is completed.

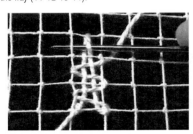
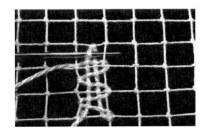
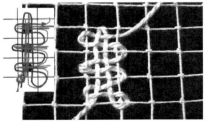

9. Pass *under* at junction 28 to access the last horizontal row. Junctions 29-30-31-32.

10. Complete the *return* on the last horizontal row. Junctions 33-34-35-36

11. The pattern is now completed.

THE HORIZONTAL ROW

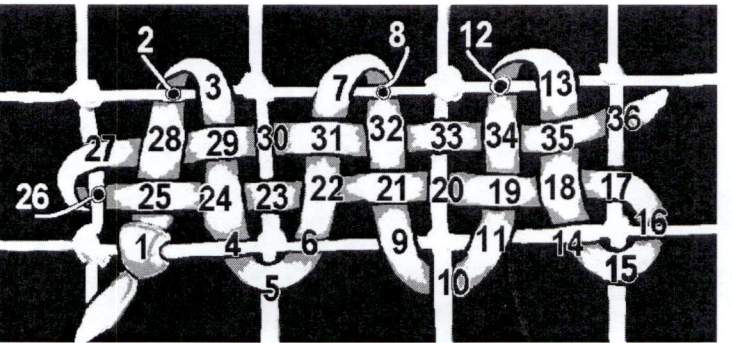

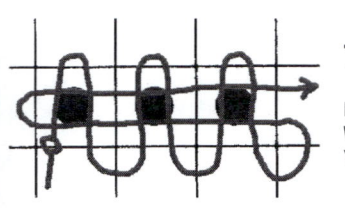

Like the vertical row, when dots are consecutive it is called a "row". It is done by going as far as possible before changing direction.

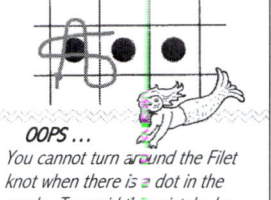

THE PATTERN

Reproduce this 3-dot pattern on your ¼" graph paper and draw this path using a pencil. When the path is finished, pass over with a colored ink pen. Then erase the pencil marks. Your pattern will be ready for embroidery.

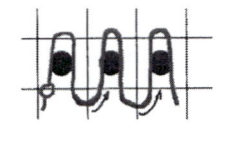 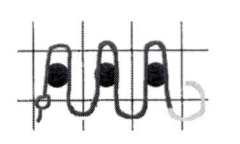 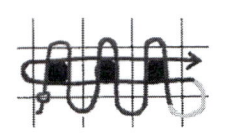 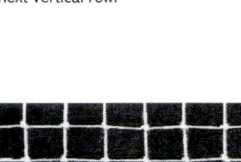

1. Make a circle that represents the beginning of your pattern (and the *Temporary knot* on the filet net)
Complete one vertical row on the first mesh (Key No. 2).

2. To reach the second dot, draw a scallop.
You are now in position for the next vertical row.

3. Complete each vertical row taking care to draw the scallop away from the corner (the Filet knot) and to leave a nice sized loop at the top.
You have now completed the entire vertical row of dots available.

4. Because there are no more vertical rows (dots) on the right side, it is time to *change direction by turning around the small Filet knot.*
This action puts you in position to draw the horizontal row.

5. Do the horizontal row and the parallel *return*. Finish with an arrow to show the end of this pattern.

OOPS ...
You cannot turn around the Filet knot when there is a dot in the mesh. To avoid this mistake be sure to draw your 'changes of direction' with a large motion as it will be easier to see the mistake.

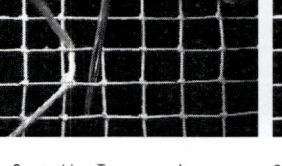  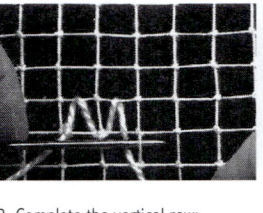  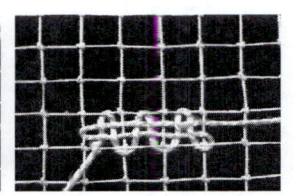

1. Start with a Temporary knot on junction 1.
Going up, do a vertical row with junction 2 —the needle passes *under*. (Key No. 1)
Complete this vertical row: the thread folds *over* junction 3 and the needle passes *under* junction 4. (Key No. 2)

2. To reach the other mesh on the right, the thread passes *over* junction 5.
Start next mesh under - junction 6, then *over* - junction 7.

3. Complete the vertical row: going down, fold the thread passing the needle *under* junction 8 and *over* junction 9.
Pass *under* junction 10 to reach the other mesh on the right.

4. Complete this last mesh: *over* junction 11, *under* junction 12, fold the thread *over* junction 13, and *under* at junction 14.
Change direction around the small Filet knot: the thread passes *over* junction 15 and *under* junction 16.

5. You are now in position to start the horizontal row. Weave the needle through the whole row at once and count every thread on your way; place your needle *over* junction 17. You should finish with *Under* at junction 26. This is the first part of the horizontal row.

6. Holding the needle with your left hand, in one motion, complete the *return*. This is the second part of the horizontal row (by weaving junctions 27 to 36). Your horizontal row is now completed.

A SQUARE

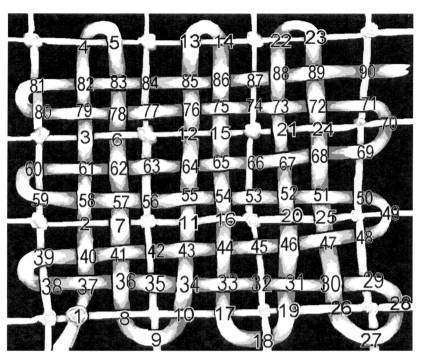

THE PATTERN

This square has 3 consecutive vertical rows. When there are no more vertical rows on the right, it is time to *change direction*, to draw the horizontal rows.

Reproduce this pattern on your ¼" graph paper. Start the Path with a Temporary knot on the bottom of the chosen mesh (Key No. 1)

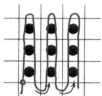 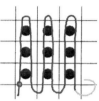 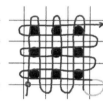 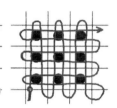

1. Draw 3 consecutive vertical rows. Each row is 3 dots high.
When there are no more vertical rows at the same level, it is time to *change direction*.

2. *Change direction* by turning around the little knot of the filet net. Draw this turn in a large motion.

3. Then draw the 3 horizontal rows. Each horizontal row is 3 dots long.

4. Draw the line further at the junction of the filet and an arrow to show the end of the Path.

THE EMBROIDERY

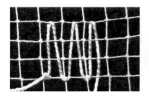 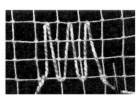 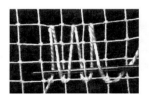 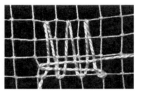 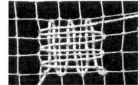 

1. With your pencil, follow your pattern and reproduce these 3 vertical rows, from junction 1 (the Temporary knot) to junction 26 *under* (the return on the last vertical row).

2. *Change direction by turning around the small knot of the filet net* (junctions 27 *over* & 28 *under*).

3. Start the first part of the horizontal rows with the needle *over* at junction 29 to *under* at junction 38.

4. Complete the Return of the row (Key No. 2) from *over* junction 39 to *under* junction 48.
Go to the next row: Pass *over* at junction 49

5. Repeat as many times as there are horizontal rows to be done at the same level. (Through to junction 90). Verify the accuracy of the weaving.

OOPS ...
There is an error in weaving: The *Under / Over* order has not been maintained. Good light is important as well as a dark background fabric.

THE DIAGONAL

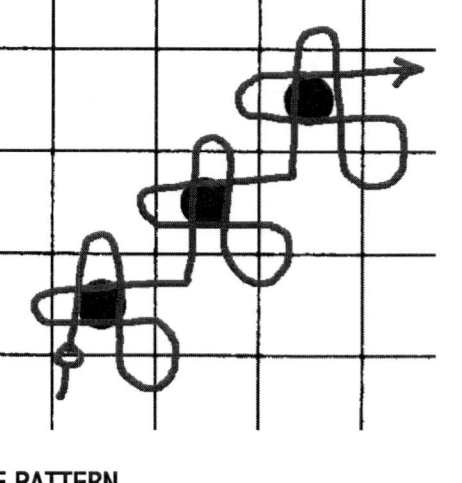

CHANGES OF DIRECTION

There are two ways to *change direction* from going vertically or horizontally.

No. 1: "CHANGE DIRECTION BY TURNING AROUND THE SMALL KNOT OF THE FILET NET"

In the preceding exercises, we have learned how to Change Direction to complete the horizontal row: by drawing an oversized loop around the corner of the filet knot we were able to go from a vertical row to a horizontal row.

No. 2: "CHANGE DIRECTION WITH A RIGHT ANGLE"

This Change of Direction is used when the dot is in a diagonal position with another dot. In more elaborate patterns, this change of direction will be easy to recognize when you acquire the good habit of drawing the line a bit longer, beyond the filet net line.

THE PATTERN

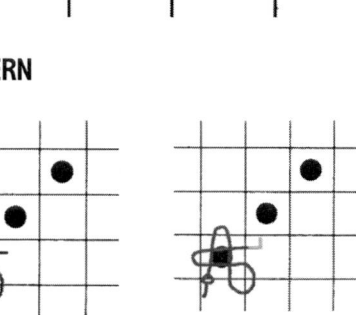

1. Start with a temporary knot.
Draw the path
of this 1st dot:
- A vertical row,
- *Change direction No. 1* ...
around the small knot of the
filet net;
- A horizontal row.
Because there are no more
dots at the same level, we need
to change direction.

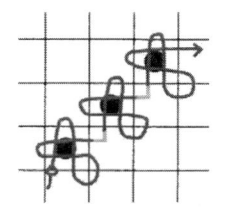

2. *Change direction No. 2*
...with a *right angle*: draw a
right angle going up.

You are now ready to start the
other mesh:
- A vertical row;
- *Change direction No. 1* ... by
turning around the small knot
of the filet net;
- A horizontal row.

3. Because there are no more
rows to do at this level, *change
direction* and draw another
complete mesh (vertical and
horizontal).

Repeat until there are no more
dots to be filled.

4. This horizontal row is now
completed.

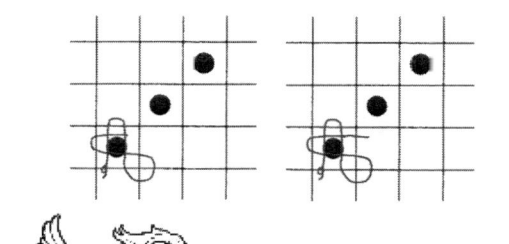

ACQUIRE THE GOOD HABIT

*When making a path, do not stop before the end
of the row* (See "Basics of the Linen Stitch — Let's be accurate"). *Be sure
you are drawing your line slightly further, beyond the grid line. Doing this
step will help you make the choice of the next "Change of Direction".*

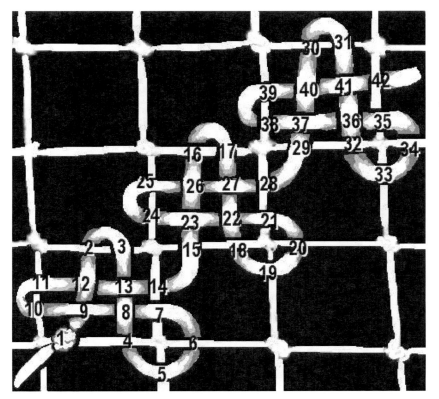

THE EMBROIDERY ON THE FILET NET

FOLLOW THE JUNCTIONS

- Junctions 1 to 4 is for the complete vertical row;

- Junctions 5 and 6 is for the *Change of direction No.1;*

- Junction 7-8-9-10-11-12-13 & 14 is for the complete horizontal row;

- The *Change of direction No. 2 (with the right angle)* is located just between junctions 14 and 15; junction 14 is the end of the horizontal row and junction 15 is the beginning of the vertical row.

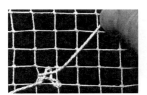  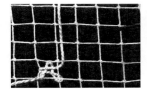 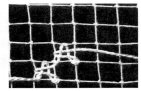 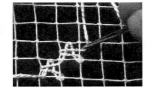 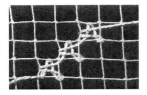

1. Complete a vertical row from junctions 1 through 4 *(under)*. *Change direction No. 1 ...around the Filet knot* on junctions 5 *over* and 6 *under* and complete the horizontal row from junction 7 *over* to 14 *under*.

2. *Change direction No. 2 ...with a right angle*, and prepare to do the vertical row on the second mesh. Position your needle going up, passing *over* junction 15 and *under* at junction 16.

3. Complete the *return* on this vertical row passing *over junction* 17 and *under* junction 18.

4. *Change direction No. 1 ...turning around the small knot of the filet. over* on junction 19 and *under* on junction 20.
Then, complete a horizontal row from junction 21 *(over)* to junction 28 *(under)*.

5. *Change Direction No. 2 ...with a right angle* (the needle shows the position of the right angle). Complete the last mesh: from junction 29 *(over) to* junction 32 *(under)*.
Change direction No. 1 at junction 33 *(over)* & junction 34 *(under)*.

6. Complete the horizontal row (junction 35 *over* to junction 42 *under*).

EXERCISES – THE LINEN STITCH

EXERCISE 1

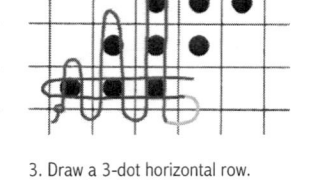

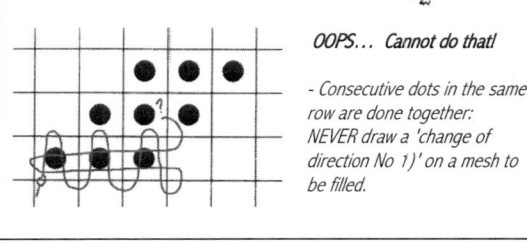

OOPS... Cannot do that!

- Consecutive dots in the same row are done together: NEVER draw a 'change of direction No 1)' on a mesh to be filled.

1. There are 3 consecutive vertical rows at the same level.

2. There are no more vertical rows to do at this level so, *Change direction No.1 ... by turning around the small knot of the filet net.*

3. Draw a 3-dot horizontal row. Note that the line you are drawing is going beyond the grid line.

4. *Change Direction No. 2 ...with a right angle.* Prepare to do the upward vertical row.

5. Draw a 2-dot vertical row. *Change direction No. 1.* Draw a 3-dot horizontal row. Prepare to *Change direction No. 2 ...with a right angle* to do the one-dot vertical row.

6. Draw the 1-dot vertical row. *Change direction No. 1* and draw the 3-dot horizontal row to complete the pattern.

EXERCISE 2

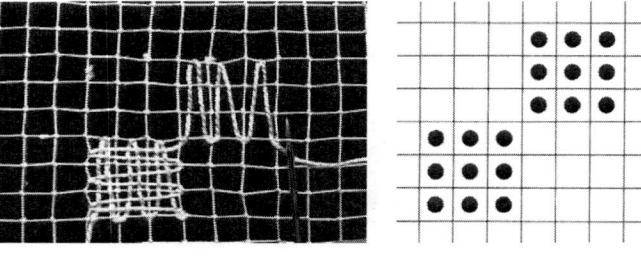

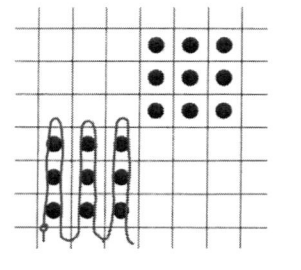

1. This first square has three 3-dot consecutive vertical rows, each at the same level.

2. When there are no more vertical rows at the same level, *Change direction No.1)* and draw the horizontal rows.

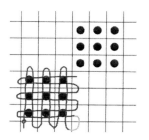
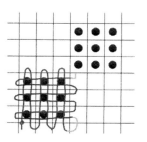
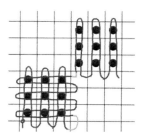
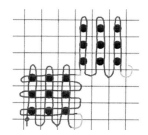
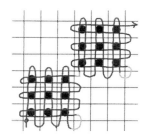

3. There are 3 horizontal rows of 3 dots each.

4. There are no more horizontal rows to draw at this same level. *Change direction No. 2 ...with a right angle.*

5. Complete these 3 consecutive vertical rows.

6. *Change direction.*

7. Draw the 3 consecutive horizontal rows to complete the pattern.

EXERCISE 3

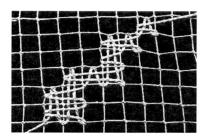
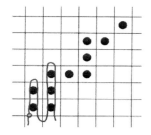
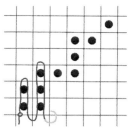
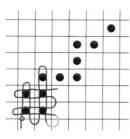

1. Draw a Temporary knot. Draw 2 vertical rows: one is 2 dots high and the second is a 3 dot row.

2. There are no more vertical rows at the same level, so use the *change direction No. 1 ...around the small knot of the filet net.*

3. Complete 2 horizontal rows. These rows have 2 dots each.

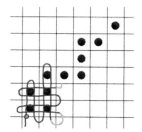
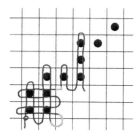
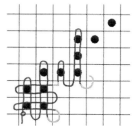
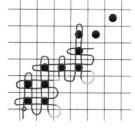
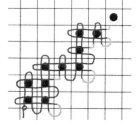
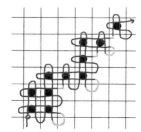

4. *Change direction No. 2 ...with a right angle* going up.

5. Draw 2 vertical rows: one is 1 dot high and the second is 3 dots high.

6. *Change direction* for this 3 dot horizontal row.

7. Complete 2 horizontal rows: one is a 3 dot row and the second is a 1 dot row.

8. *Change direction No. 2 ...with a right angle* and complete a 1 dot vertical row and a 2 dot horizontal row.

9. *Change direction No. 1* to complete the single dot. Exit with an arrow to mark the end of this path.

PROJECT LEVEL 1 – THE LINEN STITCH

GEOMETRIC PATTERN

This project has 9 individual geometric shapes.

ON THE PAPER

1. Reproduce these patterns on your ¼" grid paper, respecting the location of each dot / shape on the page.

2. With your pencil handy, study the completed pattern bellow, then hide the page and do not peak at it while doing your exercise.

3. Open your book to the Keys page and use Keys No. 1 & No. 2, with the *changes of directions No 1 and No.2.*

4. Draw the paths of these 9 patterns, first with a pencil then with the ink pen as explained in Chapter 2. Do not turn the page while doing the paths: keep your page in the same position during the whole exercise.

ON THE FILET NET

5. Prepare a needle with approximately 2 yards/meters of thread.

6. Count the holes on your filet net so you have enough room to do the whole project. If your previous exercises are taking too much room, reposition your filet net on the frame.

7. Start with the lowest pattern on the left. Position the *Temporary knot* at the proper place on your filet net.

8. Follow your pattern with a pencil, one step at a time and reproduce this step on the netting. Carefully count all the *Under / Over* motions for the perfect weaving of the Linen Stitch. If there is a mistake, undo and redo.

9. Do not turn your frame while doing the whole embroidery.

10. Use the *Permanent Knots* when needed during the work (Refer to Chapter 1-General Directions).

11. When one path is finished, leave 3" of thread at the back of the work.

If the weaving in the large square is not perfect, redo the exercise on the filet net as many times as it takes to make it perfect. Correct the lighting for your eyes, and be sure to have a dark fabric on the back of your frame (Refer to "Environment" in Chapter 1, General Directions).

COMPLETED PATH FOR PROJECT LEVEL 1

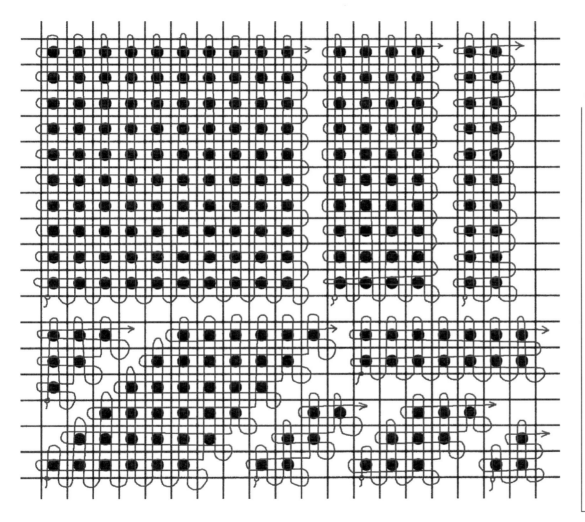

A QUICK WAY TO VERIFY THE ACCURACY OF THE LINEN STITCH

At the top of the picture, look at the two rows on each side of the filet net thread (bb). These two threads must be mirrored:

- the thread folds "over",
- there is the knot of the filet net, and
- the thread passes "over" on the next row.

As at the bottom of the picture, the over / under alternates: one goes over and the next one goes under and the third one goes over, etc.

(bb)   (cc)

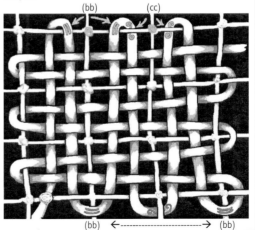

(bb) ←-------------------→ (bb)

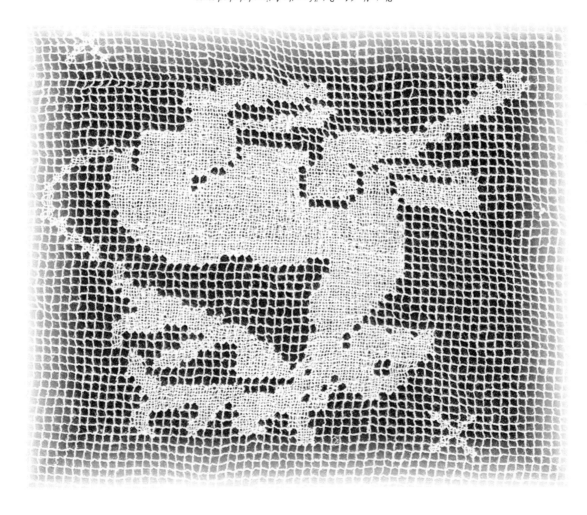

CHAPTER 4
LEVEL 2 – THE HIDDEN STITCH

GOALS for LEVEL 2

~ Know how to use Keys No. 1 No. 2 and No. 3 ~
~ Be comfortable navigating the Path with the two "Changes of Direction" ~
~ Know how to count the Under / Over motions combined with the Hidden Stitch ~

Reach these goals before starting Level 3

BASICS of the HIDDEN STITCH

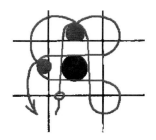

The Hidden Stitch is used with the Linen Stitch to conceal the thread:

- To soften an edge of loops, balance a motif and reach the *Temporary knot.*
- To reach other sections on the design without cutting the thread.

The change of direction to pass from the horizontal row to the Hidden Stitch is done exactly as when we change direction from a vertical row to a horizontal row (See "Basics of the Linen Stitch in chapter 3).

THE PATTERN – DRAW THE PATH

On paper, the Hidden Stitch is a large dot, as large as the dot in the middle of the mesh. It fills the whole space on the top of the loop over the line of the filet net. When your pattern is finished, the lines of the path are done with the colored ink, so the Hidden Stitch cannot be confused with the black dot. Using the template to learn the proportion, draw this one-dot pattern.

1. ONE DOT
Reproduce this single dot on your ¼" graph paper and draw the path as you have learned.

2. CHANGING DIRECTION
Change Direction No. 1 to reach the tip of the upper loop. *(Change Direction by turning around the small knot of the filet net).*

3. HIDDEN STITCH
Draw a big round dot that will fill the whole space of the loop between the tip and the line of the graph paper.

4. CHANGING DIRECTION
Change Direction No. 1 to reach the other loop *(change direction by turning around the little knot of the filet net).*

5. HIDDEN STITCH
Draw another big dot to mark the Hidden Stitch on this loop.

6. REACH THE STARTING POINT
and draw a small arrow to identify the end of the path.

THE EMBROIDERY ON THE FILET NET

Like the weaving of the Linen Stitch, the Hidden Stitch follows the rules of weaving: alternating the *Under, Over, Under* motion. It is done only on the tip of a loop as shown on the picture at the right.

The stitch has two actions: the ENTRY of the needle and the EXIT of the needle.
Each action is counted individually for the weaving to coincide.

The arrow on the illustration (at the left) shows the ENTRY of the Hidden Stitch (the thread passes *Over*) and the EXIT (the thread passes *Under*).

But the sequence is not always in this order: in the next pattern (Hidden Stitch on a Vertical Row) you will see that it is not always *Entry-Over / Exit-Under,* sometime it is *Entry-Under / Exit-Over.* It depends on the location of the thread just before making a Hidden Stitch.

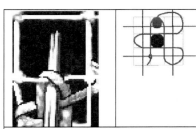

On this example, the needle enters the loop which includes the filet net thread.

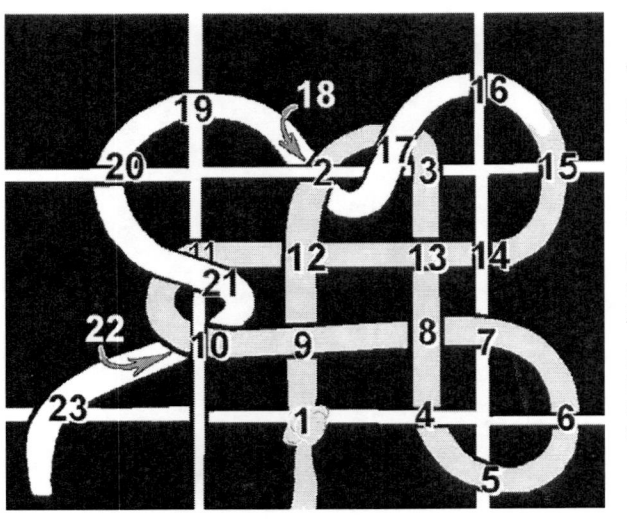

THE HIDDEN STITCH COMBINED WITH THE LINEN STITCH IS SIMPLE

Knowing that the Hidden Stitch counts for 2 actions, the weaving with the Linen Stitch is simple: alternate the *Under / Over* without leaving this order.

Follow the numbered picture on the left with the table on your right to understand the two-action Hidden Stitch. Speak out loud at each junction starting with junction 1 – the Temporary knot.

It is important to be accurate in the counting of the *Under / Over* of the Hidden Stitch as many mistakes are made at this level. Falling out of this regularity will produce an error and the weave in the rest of your work will not be accurate.

TABLE – FOLLOW THE PATH

This table is the written actions of the Hidden Stitch starting with a complete mesh in Linen Stitch.

Junction 14	UNDER filet net thread
Junction 15	OVER filet net thread
Junction 16	UNDER filet net thread
Junction 17	OVER – ENTRY Hidden Stitch
Junction 18	UNDER – EXIT Hidden Stitch
Junction 19	OVER filet net thread
Junction 20	UNDER filet net thread
Junction 21	OVER – ENTRY Hidden Stitch
Junction 22	UNDER – EXIT Hidden Stitch
Junction 23	OVER filet net thread

FOLLOW THE PATTERN STEP-BY-STEP

Complete the one-mesh pattern and then follow the step-by-step directions. At junction 14, your thread should be *Under.*

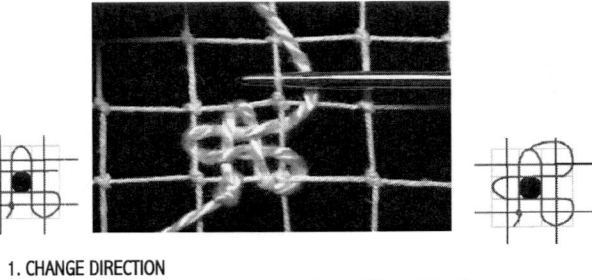

1. CHANGE DIRECTION
Change Direction No. 1 by turning around the small knot of the filet net to reach the tip of the loop.
Over junction 15
Under junction 16

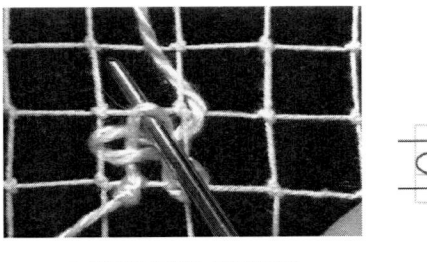

2. HIDDEN STITCH - THE ENTRY
OVER at junction 17

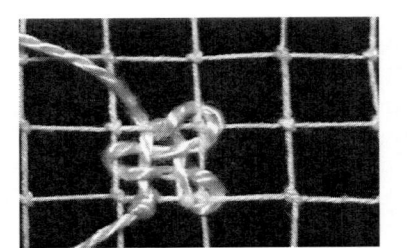

3. HIDDEN STITCH - THE EXIT
Under at junction 18

The needle enters at junction 17 and exits at junction 13.
This is one complete Hidden Stitch

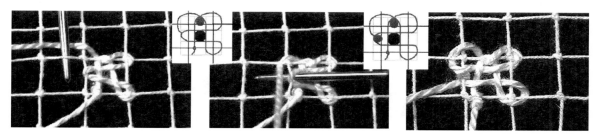

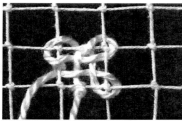

4. CHANGE DIRECTION by turning around the small knot of the filet net.
Junction19 is *OVER* and junction 20 is *UNDER*.

5. HIDDEN STITCH - THE ENTRY
OVER at junction 21.

The needle enters at junction 21 and exits at junction 22.
Remember, it takes 2 actions to make a complete Hidden Stitch.

6. HIDDEN STITCH - THE EXIT
UNDER at junction 22.

7. CHANGE DIRECTION
to reach the Temporary knot:
OVER junction 23.

Check the tension: each time you are making a Hidden Stitch, be sure to pull the thread sufficiently so that it is well placed and follows the edge.

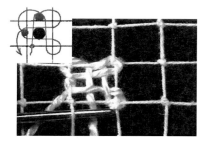

8. TO REACH THE BEGINNING OF YOUR WORK
UNDER. This is junction 24.

Undo the Temporary knot at junction 1 and finish: tie a Finishing knot at the back, in the middle of the mesh (as explained in Chapter 1).

Photo 15: Detail of a square from the Antique Baby Bed Cover

HIDDEN STITCH on a VERTICAL ROW

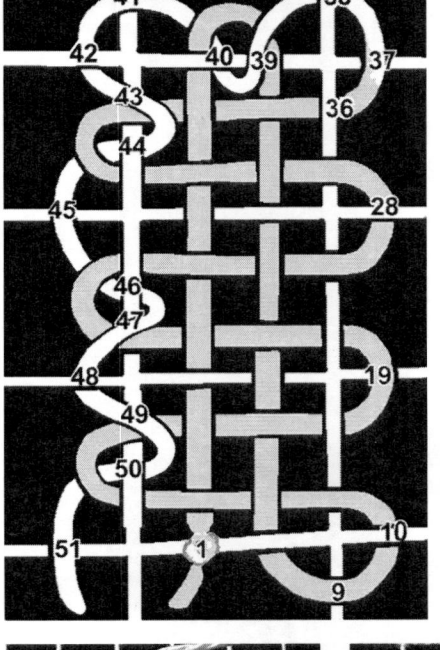

PATH ON THE PATTERN

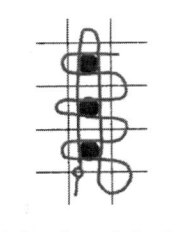 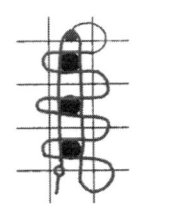 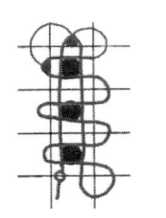 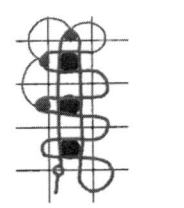 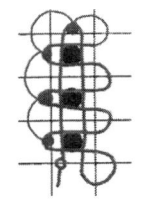 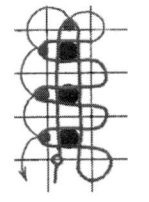

1. Draw the vertical and horizontal rows of your pattern.

2. *Change direction No. 1* and reach the loop of the vertical row and form one Hidden Stitch.

3. Draw a large curve to *change direction No. 1* and draw a large dot on the other loop on the horizontal row.

4. Draw a scallop to reach the other tip and draw a Hidden Stitch.

5. Repeat the Hidden Stitch. Be sure the dot fills the whole tip of the loop as shown.

6. Draw the line with the arrow that will mark the end of this path.

EMBROIDERY ON THE FILET NET

Do we start the Hidden Stitch *Over* or *Under*? --- The Hidden Stitch does not always have its Entry with an Over. It depends on the last position of the thread. You must respect the ultimate rule of the weaving: the *Under / Over* must always be consecutive on each thread/junction your needle is meeting on the path of your pattern.

COMPARE HIDDEN STITCHES	Junctions 43 & 44	Junctions 46 & 47
Because the previous junction is	Under at junction 42	Over at junction 45
The Entry of the Hidden Stitch is	Over	Under

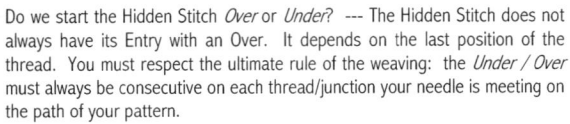

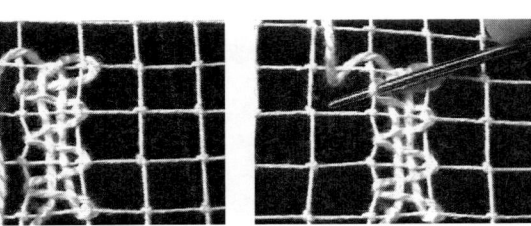

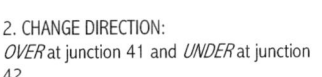

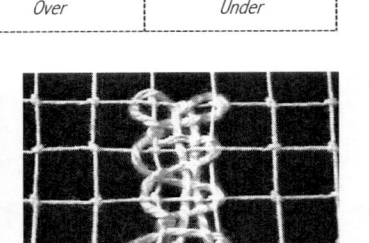

6. Start with a 3-mesh vertical row. The horizontal row finishes *UNDER* at junction 36.
Change of direction No. 1:
OVER junction 37, *UNDER* junction 38
HIDDEN STITCH:
ENTRY is *OVER* junction 39, and EXIT is *UNDER* junction 40.
(Keep the thread away from the needle to avoid making a knot while pulling the threaded needle.)

2. CHANGE DIRECTION:
OVER at junction 41 and *UNDER* at junction 42.

(Your thread is now *UNDER*, so the next junction would be *OVER*)

.

3. Hidden Stitch:
Entry is *OVER* at junction 43.
Exit is *UNDER* at junction 44.

4. Pass *OVER* the filet net thread at junction 45.

HIDDEN STITCH:
This hidden stitch has its entry *UNDER* junction 46 and the exit is *OVER* junction 47.

(Look at the position of the needle: with your left hand, hold the needle in the same direction as the row with the loop. Pull the needle with the right hand.)

5. Pass *UNDER* junction 48

HIDDEN STITCH:
Entry *OVER* junction 49;
Exit *UNDER* junction 50.

OVER junction 51 and *UNDER* the next filet net thread to reach junction 1.

HIDDEN STITCH on a HORIZONTAL ROW

DRAW THE PATH ON THE PATTERN

TABLE — FOLLOW THE PATH	
Junction 36	UNDER the filet net
Junction 37	OVER-Change Direction
Junction 38	UNDER — Change Direction
Junction 39	OVER — Entry of the Hidden Stitch
Junction 40	UNDER-Exit of the Hidden Stitch
Junction 41	OVER the filet net
Junction 42	UNDER —Entry of the Hidden Stitch
Junction 43	OVER — Exit of the Hidden Stitch
Junction 44	UNDER the filet net
Junction 45	OVER — Entry of the Hidden Stitch
Junction 46	UNDER — Exit of the Hidden Stitch
Junction 47	OVER — Change Direction
Junction 48	UNDER — Change of Direction
Junction 49	OVER — Entry of the Hidden Stitch
Junction 50	UNDER — Exit of the Hidden Stitch
Junction 51	OVER the filet net to reach the knot

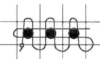 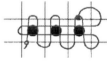 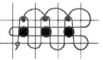 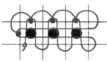 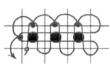

1. Start with a Temporary knot; then draw the path of this horizontal row from junction 1 to junction 36.

2. *Change direction No. 1* to reach the tip of the loop. Draw a Hidden Stitch.

3. Draw a scallop over the line of the filet net to reach the other loop, and place a Hidden Stitch on the tip of the second loop.

4. Draw as many Hidden Stitches as necessary to reach the Temporary knot. Separate them by a large scallop.

5. End your pattern with a small arrow.

FOLLOW THE PATH ON THE FILET NET

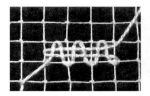  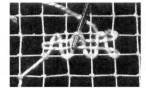   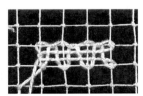

1. Complete a 3-mesh horizontal row from junction 1 ending *Under* at junction 36.

2. CHANGE DIRECTION No. 1: *Over* (37) *Under* (38).
HIDDEN STITCH: Entry *Over* (39); Exit Under (40).

3. OVER junction 41.
HIDDEN STITCH: *Under* (entrance on junction 42) *Over* (exit on 43).

4. *Under* junction 44
HIDDEN STITCH entry *Over* (45). Exit *Under* (46).

5. CHANGE DIRECTION: *Over* (47) *Under* (48).
HIDDEN STITCH: Entry *Over* (49) Exit *Under* (50)

6. *Over* junction 51... to complete the pattern. Undo the Temporary knot, reweave and make the Finishing knot

HIDDEN STITCH on a DIAGONAL

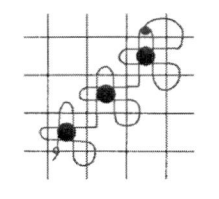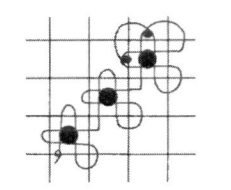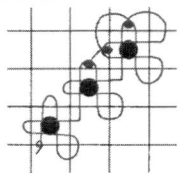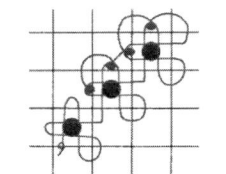

The Hidden Stitch is used here to conceal the thread while reaching the Temporary Knot.

On the pattern, the Hidden stitch is the large dot that fills the loop of the Linen Stitch already in place. When 2 Hidden Stitches are consecutive, like at junctions 50 and 51, draw a straight line between; no curved line here!

On the Filet Net, as usual, the sequence of the *Under / Over* must alternate each time your needle meets another thread / junction. (Look at the table to follow the sequence.)

Take a closer look at Junctions 49-50 and junctions 51-52:
- The entry for the Hidden Stitch at junction 49 is *Over* because the last junction (48) is *Under*.
- Because the junction 50 is *Under*, the junction 51 is *Over* (Entry of the Hidden Stitch).

TABLE – SEQUENCE OF THE PATH	
Junction 43	OVER – *Change of direction*
Junction 44	UNDER –*Change of direction*
Junction 45	OVER – *Entry of the Hidden Stitch*
Junction 46	UNDER – *Exit of the Hidden Stitch*
Junction 47	OVER – *Change of Direction*
Junction 48	UNDER – *Change of Direction*
Junction 49	OVER – *Entry of the Hidden Stitch*
Junction 50	UNDER – *Exit of the Hidden Stitch*
Junction 51	OVER – *Entry of the Hidden Stitch*
Junction 52	UNDER – *Exit of the Hidden Stitch*
Junction 53	OVER – *Change of Direction ...*

DRAW THE PATH

1. Complete a 3 dot diagonal. Change direction No. 1 to reach the loop and apply a Hidden Stitch.

2. Change Direction No. 1 to reach the other tip of the loop.

3. To reach the other loop, draw a direct line between the two hidden stitches (no curved line here).

4. Change direction No. 1 to draw another Hidden Stitch.

5. ...and so on until you have reached the end. Draw an arrow.

FOLLOW THE PATH ON THE FILET NET

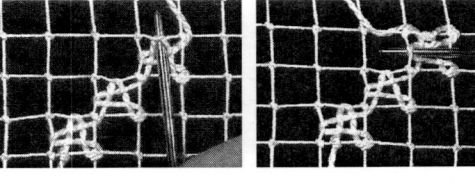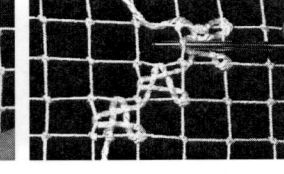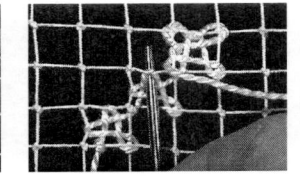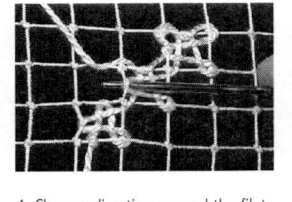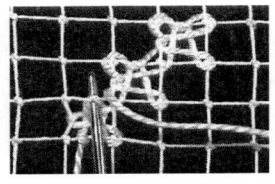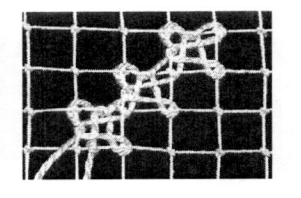

1. Complete this diagonal (*Under* at Junction 42).
Change direction: 43 *Over* & 44 *Under*. Hidden Stitch: *Over* 45, *Under* junction 46.

2. Change direction around the filet knot (47 *Over* & 48 *Under*). This Hidden Stitch in the horizontal loop is *Over* at junction 49 and *Under* at junction 50.

3. The next Hidden Stitch goes directly to the other loop at junction 51, *Over* and at junction 52 *Under*.

4. Change direction around the filet knot (53 & 54) and work a Hidden Stitch on the horizontal loop — junction 55 *Over and* at junction 56 *Under*.

5. This Hidden Stitch goes directly from one loop to the other.

6. Change direction to reach the other loop and do another Hidden Stitch. Verify the *Under/Over* of your Hidden Stitch to be sure of the order.

EXERCISES – THE HIDDEN STITCH

EXERCISE 1 – A SIMPLE SQUARE BORDER

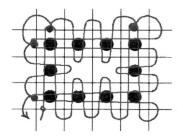

This 4-sided border can be done in many ways.
This is the easiest way to do it with what you know so far.

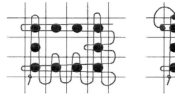 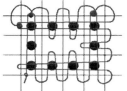

    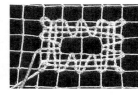 

1. Follow the pattern, changing direction when needed.
The Change of direction is *Under, Over.*
The Hidden Stitch is *Under + Over.*

2. *Under* the thread of the filet net. Two consecutive one-mesh vertical rows.

3. *Under the* thread of the filet net. Hidden Stitch: *Over +Under.*

4. Change direction: *Over, Under.* Hidden Stitch: *Over + Under*

5. *Over* the thread of the filet net. One-mesh vertical row: *Under, Over, Under, Over, Under, Over, Under, Over.*
Under the vertical thread of the filet net.

6. *Over* the thread of the filet net ... to reach the Temporary knot.

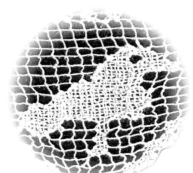 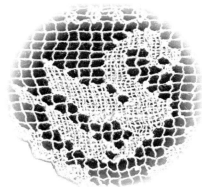 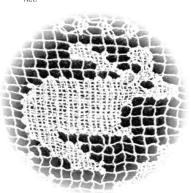

Photo 16 – Three motifs from the border of the Antique baby bed cover

EXERCISE 2 — A BORDER ON 3 SIDES

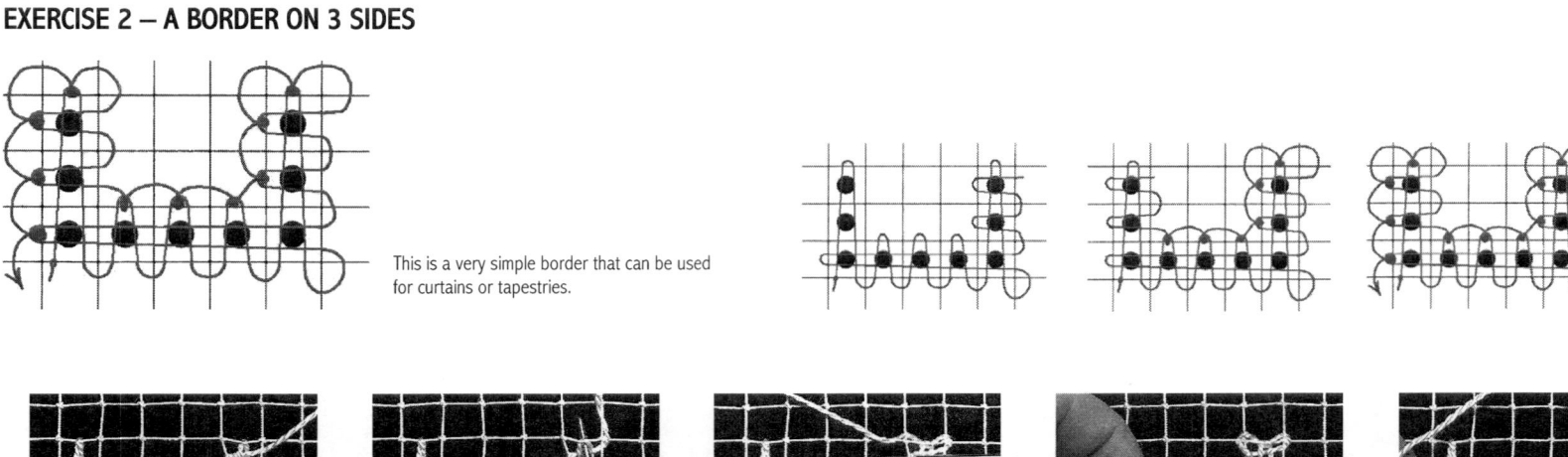

This is a very simple border that can be used for curtains or tapestries.

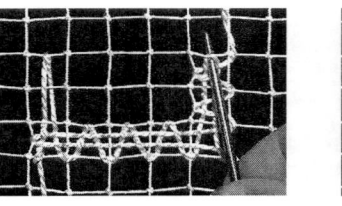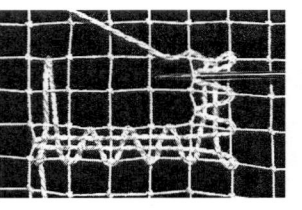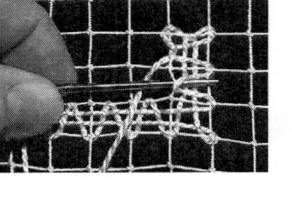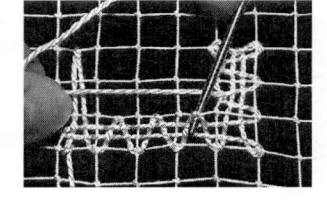

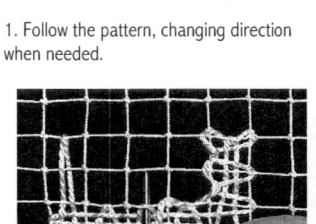

1. Follow the pattern, changing direction when needed.

2. Change direction: *Over, Under*. Hidden Stitch: *Over + Under*.

3. Change direction: *Over + Under*. Hidden Stitch: *Over + Under*.

4. *Over* the thread of the filet net. Hidden Stitch: *Under + Over*.

5. Direct Hidden stitch from one loop to another: *Under + Over*.

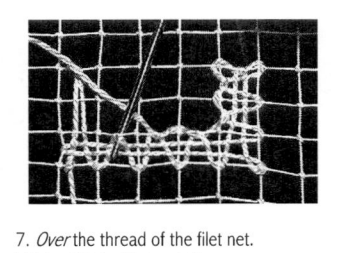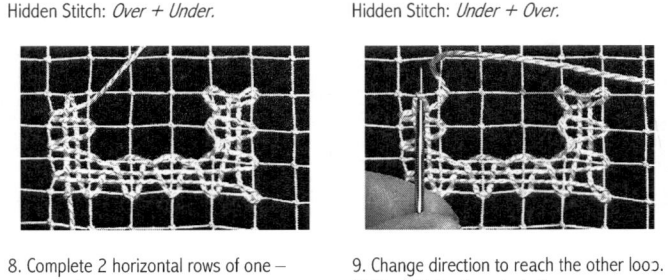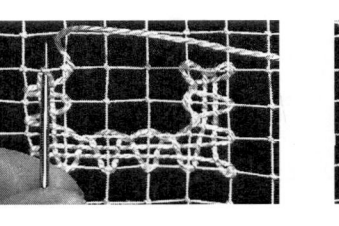

6. Pass *Under* the thread of the filet net. Hidden Stitch: *Over + Under*.

7. *Over* the thread of the filet net. Hidden Stitch: *Under + Over*.

8. Complete 2 horizontal rows of one — mesh each.

9. Change direction to reach the other loop. Hidden Stitch: *Over + Under*.

10. Change direction: *Over* and then *Under*.

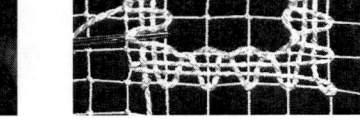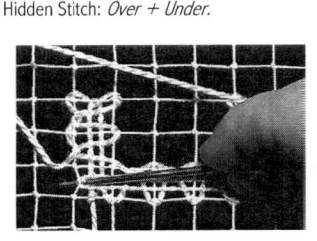

11. Hidden Stitch: *Over + Under*.

12. Pass *Over* the thread of the filet net. Hidden Stitch: *Under + Over*.

13. *Under* the filet net thread to reach the other loop.

14. Hidden Stitch on the loop: *Over + Under*.

15. Change direction to reach the Temporary knot: *Over, Under*.

EXERCISE 3 - TRIANGULAR SHAPE

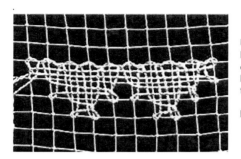

Use the Hidden Stitch to reach other part on the pattern.
It helps you reach the dots that increase and decrease the triangular shape.
It also brings you to the beginning of your work to make the Finishing knot.

Repeat this pattern to make a pointed edging.

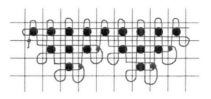 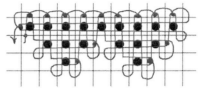

1. Complete the rows using the appropriate Changes of Direction.

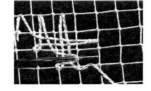

2. Hidden Stitch *Over + Under.*

3. Two-mesh vertical row
Hidden Stitch *Over + Under.*

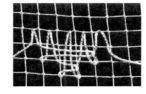

4. One-mesh vertical row.

5. A three-mesh horizontal row and a two-mesh vertical row.

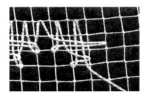

6. One-mesh horizontal row and then a 3-mesh vertical row.

7. To reach the vertical row make a Hidden Stitch: *Over + Under.*

8. A 2-mesh vertical row.
Hidden Stitch: *Over + Under.*

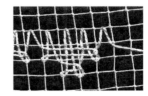

9. One-mesh vertical row.

10. With your right hand, in one motion weave the 9-mesh horizontal row.

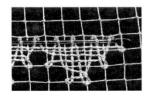

11. With your left hand, in one continuous motion, complete the Return. Your needle should end *Under* the Filet net.

12. Start a row of Hidden Stitches to soften the edge and to reach the Temporary Knot. Start the first Hidden Stitch: *Over + Under.*

13. To reach the other loop, the thread passes *Over* the Filet Net.
The Hidden Stitch on this second loop starts *Under* and exits *Over.*

14. Repeat the Hidden Stitch until you reach the Temporary knot. Carefully count the *Under/Over* on each action.

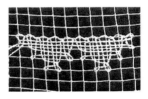

15. The Pattern is now completed. Your thread has reached the beginning of your work and you can close with a Finishing knot.

EXERCISE 4 – HEART SHAPE

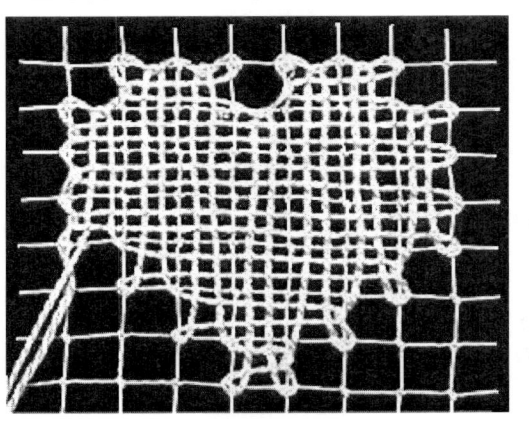

This heart shape well illustrates the function of the Hidden stitch:

- to reach other parts on the drawing;
- to visually balance the weight on both sides, and reach the starting point.

To do this embroidery, prepare a needle with 3 yards of thread.

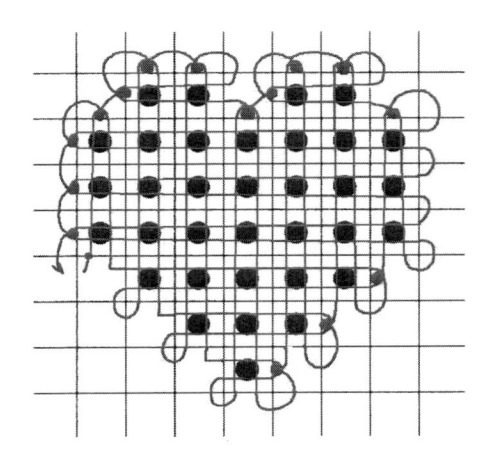

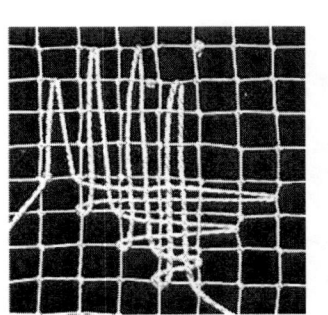

1. Follow this pattern changing direction when needed.

2. Hidden Stitch to reach the other vertical row.

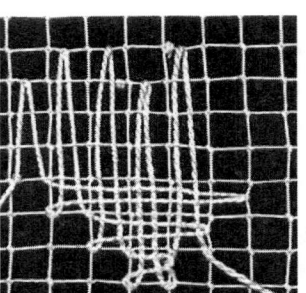

3. A 6-mesh vertical row.

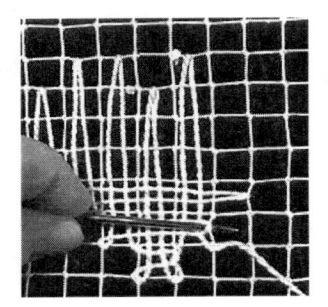

4. Hidden Stitch.

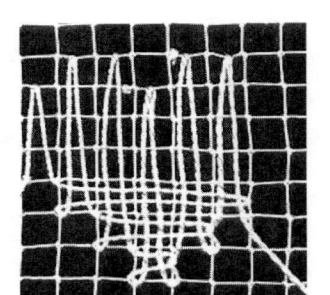

5. A 5-mesh vertical row.

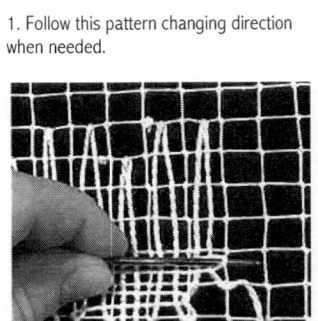

6. Hidden Stitch to reach the other row.

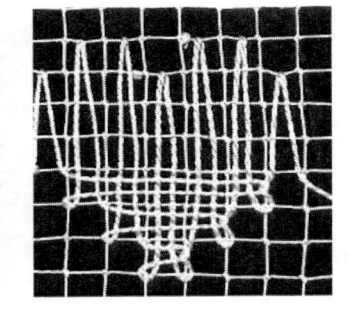

7. A 3-mesh vertical row.

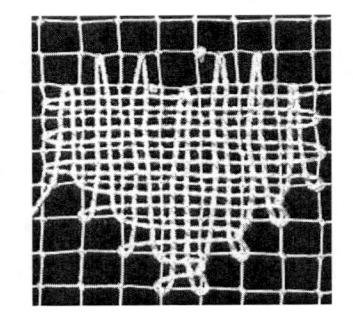

8. Change direction and complete the 7-mesh horizontal row. And repeat for the

9. Change direction to do a Hidden Stitch to reach the horizontal 2-mesh row.

10. Complete this 2-mesh horizontal row. Your thread finishes *Under*. Change

next two 7-mesh rows.

direction *Over, Under.*

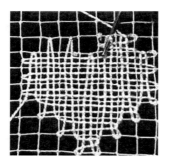

11. Hidden Stitch on the first loop is *Over + Under.*

12. *Over* the filet net thread to reach the second Hidden Stitch on this horizontal row which is *Under + Over.*

13. Change Direction (No. 1), counting all the threads your needle is meeting and do the Hidden Stitch (*Under + Over*).on the horizontal loop.

14. The next Hidden Stitch is "direct" so: *Under + Over.* This brings you to the next horizontal row.

15. Complete the horizontal 2-mesh row and change direction for 2 other Hidden Stitches

Look at your work before starting the last row of consecutive Hidden Stitches and compare.

At times, using the Hidden Stitch is a matter of esthetics. You can see how unbalanced it looks when the loops do not have the Hidden Stitches.

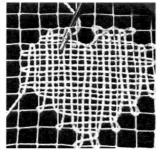
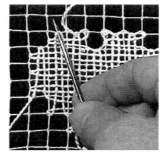

16. Hidden Stitch.

17. Another consecutive Hidden Stitch.

18. Change direction. Hidden Stitch.

19. A Direct Hidden Stitch.

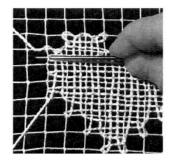
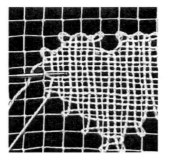

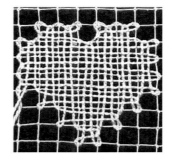
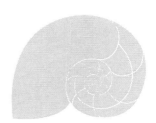

20. Change direction and start the consecutive Hidden Stitches: *Over + Under.*

21. *Over* the filet net thread. Hidden Stitch: *Under + Over.*

22. *Under* the filet net thread; Hidden Stitch *Over + Under.*

23. Change direction *Over* the filet net thread and *Under* to reach the Temporary knot.

REVIEW – THE HIDDEN STITCH

MORE EXERCISES ON PAPER

Reproduce these 8 patterns by hand on your grid paper, respecting the placement of each one on your page.
Use Keys No. 1, 2 and 3 to complete the paths.
Work the path by yourself first, and when finished, verify with the solution on the next page.
Do you need more exercises? Turn the page upside down and redo the exercises. Always start on the left side (Key No. 1).

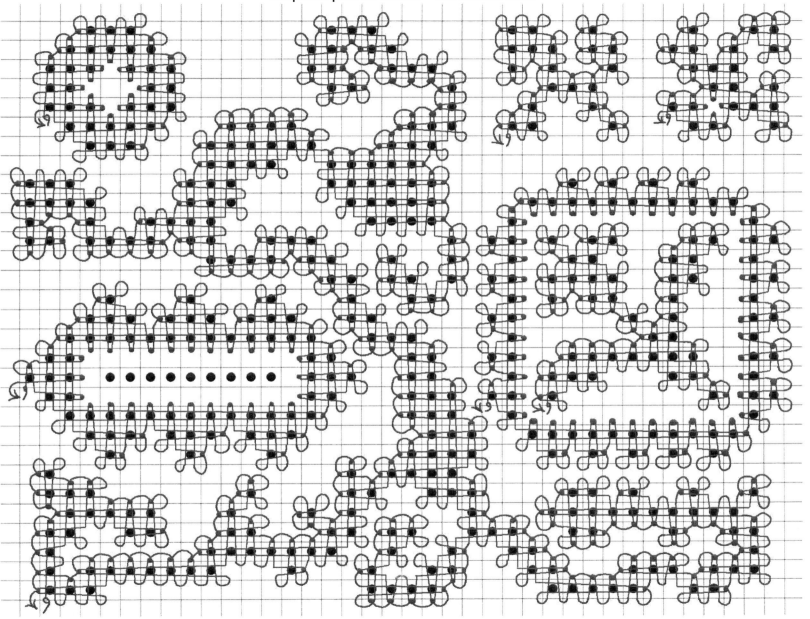

PROJECT LEVEL 2 – YOUR FIRST DOILY

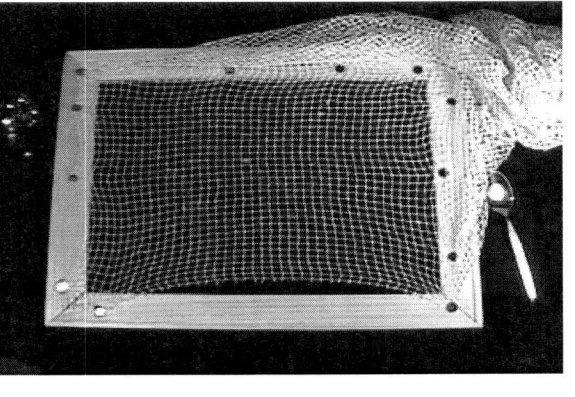

At this Level, the technique you have learned so far does not allow you to do a very large project nor an intricate lace. With this project you will learn how to add this beautiful scalloped border the easy way.

MATERIAL

- A piece of Filet Net 5 the size of your frame
- 10 grams of Coton Perlé DMC No. 5 or the equivalent
- A ballpoint needle
- A wood frame with thumbtacks or a large hoop

THE PATTERN

1. Reproduce this pattern on your graph paper. Each arrow points to the center of the pattern (see full pattern at the end of this section); the lines mark the edge where you do the Buttonhole Stitch; the small dots show you where to cut the filet net;
2. Draw the path with the pencil, using Keys No. 1, 2 and 3;
3. Trace over your path with the ink pen and erase the pencil marks;
4. Place your pattern on the table, ready to start.

EMBROIDERY ON THE FILET NET

5. Stretch a new piece of Filet Net 5 on the frame (or hoop). Be sure your pattern fits the surface by counting the meshes. Secure the excess filet net and install the contrasting background.
6. Start each Temporary knot at the right place on the filet net. Be careful not to shift the motifs/shapes: count then place the Temporary knot and count again to be sure this is the correct starting point for each shape.

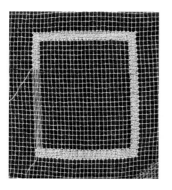 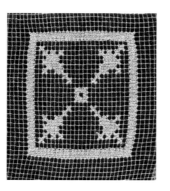   

7. Prepare your ballpoint needle with 6.5 yards of thread (6 meters), and start the embroidery of the large square. Then complete the small square in the middle.

8. Use 4 yards (3.75 meters) of thread at a time for the shapes.

9. If the thread becomes untwisted and frayed, twist it by turning your needle, or change the thread.

If the filet net is loose, tighten it.

10. When all the shapes are finished, make the Permanent knots on the back.

11. To complete your pattern with a scalloped border, you need 12 yards (11 meters) of thread. Use 6 yards (5.5 meters) at a time.

Go to section below: "Learn how to complete this outside border".

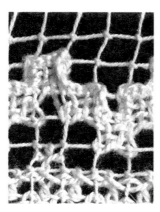 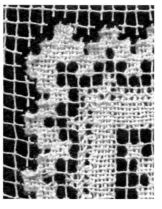 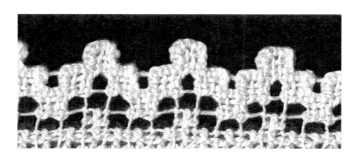

14. Wash your lace by hand. For a white lace, bleach it. Rinse twice and add a few drops of softener.

12. Use 6 yards of thread at a time to do the Buttonhole stitch on the border. Add another 6 yards when it becomes necessary. Close and hide the Permanent knot at the inside edge of the Buttonhole Stitch border (do not work any additional thread into the weaving or too close to the outside edge).

13. Cut your lace while it is still on the stretcher. Leave ¼" close to the small knots of the filet net. Notice the uncut filet thread between each scallop. The small dots on the pattern indicate where you must cut. Go slowly; if you are not sure, use a washable pen and put a mark on the filet net thread to avoid cutting the wrong filet thread.

Did you see on the edge of the inside border? There is a different stitch: this is the "Point d'Esprit", a fancy stitch that we are going to learn in another class!

15. Block your lace on the ironing board, squaring it without stretching too much and allow it to dry. Iron if necessary. You can use stainless pins to immobilize the intricate border.

LEARN HOW TO DO THE SCALLOPED BORDER

The paths of this simple border can be treated in different ways. Even though you do not have all the knowledge to be found in chapter 5, you can still create this beautiful but simple scalloped border.

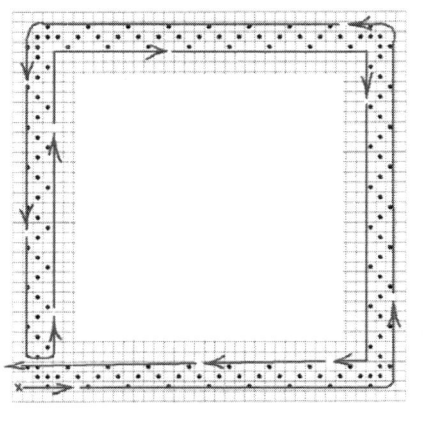

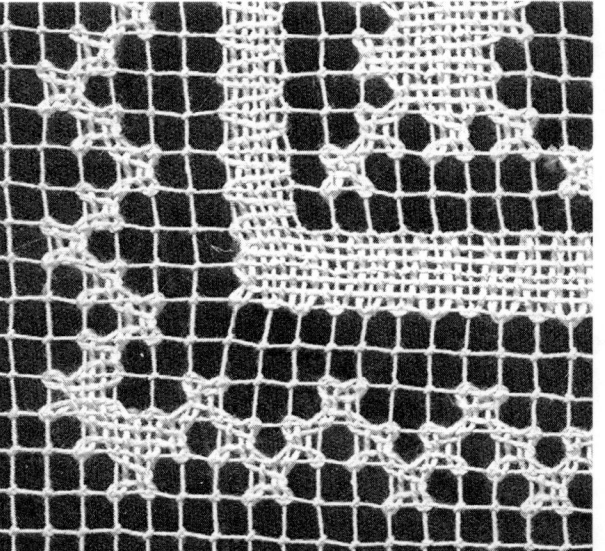

The illustration on the left gives you the general idea of the movement for this border:

1. you start drawing the outside and
2. then you draw the inside

Follow the completed pattern (on next page) and compare it with the step-by-step pictures (illustrations 1, 2 and 3 below) to guide you through this border.

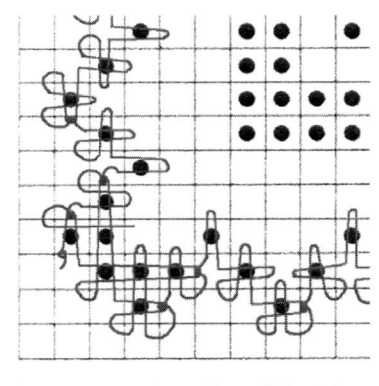

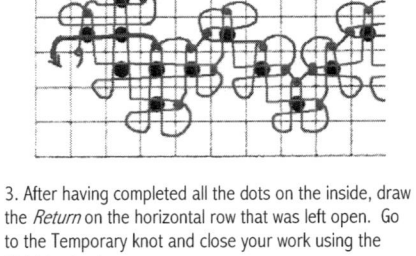

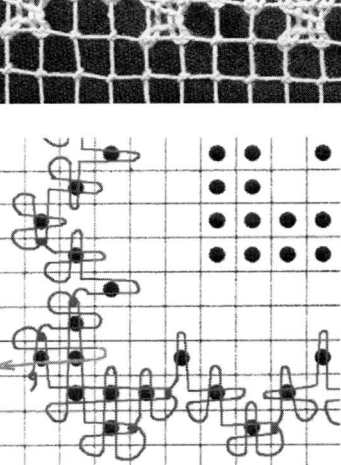

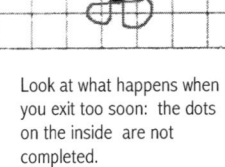

1. Start at the lower left part (Keys 1 & 2) and draw the path as you have learned.

2. Exception: At this point, do not draw the *Return* horizontal row just yet: go up and complete the dots all around the inside.

3. After having completed all the dots on the inside, draw the *Return* on the horizontal row that was left open. Go to the Temporary knot and close your work using the Finishing knot.

Look at what happens when you exit too soon: the dots on the inside are not completed.

COMPLETED PATH
FOR PROJECT
LEVEL 2 — YOUR FIRST DOILY

To be able to begin the next chapter, you must be able to complete the paths of this pattern without peeking.

Use this page only to verify the accuracy of your learning.

Photo 17 — Detail of a square from the Antique baby bed cover.

CHAPTER 5

LEVEL 3 – A POOL or A BAY

GOALS for LEVEL 3

~ *Understand and know how to use key No. 4* ~

~ *Practice the Path on many small patterns* ~

~ *Be able to draw the paths on a 40 to 50-mesh motif and gradually increase the size of your patterns* ~

Reach these goals before starting a larger project

THE POOLS AND THE BAYS

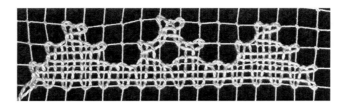

"POOL" and **"BAY"** are words to help you visualize the situation of a space which is destined to remain empty. We could have used the letter "O" for Pool and the letter "U" for Bay, but Mermie felt more comfortable referring to words of her world.

On a large and intricate design, it would be impossible to fill the entire pattern without knowing the technique to avoid going into the empty spaces; you need to know how to use Key No. 4. A Pool is not always going to be like a perfect circle: it can be an intricate shape by itself; it can also be a combination of a "Bay" inside a "Pool". Following is a concept on how to recognize empty spaces from small to very large and how to draw the Path. To better learn the technique, carefully follow these directives.

It all starts with what should be an automatic behavior from you: as soon as you start the first part of a horizontal row, going from right to left, stop everything, lift both hands and look: you have to decide if it is a "Pool" Situation or a "Bay" Situation.

THUS FAR, IN LEVEL 1 AND LEVEL 2:

1. We have learned that a row (vertical or horizontal) is composed of two threads; the first thread is the *go ahead* in the row (when you are starting your row) and the second thread is the *Return* on the row (the parallel thread that completes the row), both threads forming the loop where the Hidden Stitch goes.

2. We also now know that a mesh in Linen Stitch is the weaving of one vertical row and of one horizontal row.

3. Learning Levels 1 and 2, we have learned how to navigate the *Directions of the Path (No. 1 and No. 2)* using the first 3 keys:

    KEY No. 1 -- Always start on the left side, at the lowest row of the pattern, vertically, going up.
    KEY No. 2 -- Always complete the parallel *returns* right away on all of your horizontal / vertical rows.
    KEY No. 3 -- Use the Hidden Stitch to hide the thread and reach other groups of meshes on your pattern.

If you were to stop learning at this point, you would never be able to complete large and intricate patterns. The 4ᵗʰ Key will open the way for you to accomplish larger patterns easily. It will also require more determination and practice in doing the Paths. That is why this chapter is devoted to many kinds of paths on paper. Be persistent!

NOW IN LEVEL 3:

KEY No. 4 – This key is the exception to Key No. 2. It is used ONLY if you are starting a <u>HORIZONTAL-ROW-GOING-FROM-RIGHT-TO-LEFT</u>, and when you <u>MEET-A-POOL-SITUATION</u>. Use the Hidden Stitch (or a vertical row) to bypass the empty mesh. Do not immediately complete the *Return* on the row: continue to the left as far as possible as you meet new "Pool" situations. When there are no more "Pool" situations on the left, turn and complete all the *Returns* using the vertical row (going up) to bypass the empty mesh.

WHERE IS THE POOL?

"Pool" and "Bay" both start with a Horizontal-Row-Going-From-Right-To-Left

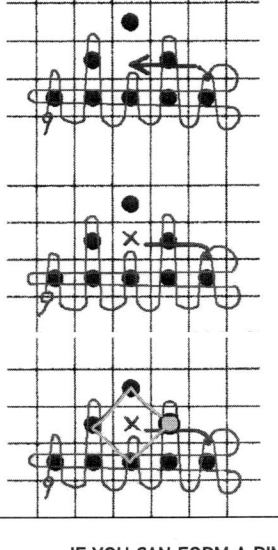

Here is the situation:

You are drawing the **first part** of a
Horizontal-Row-Going-From-Right-To-Left,
and you have an **empty space just on the left** of it
(shown with an "x").

Do not complete the *Return* on the row just yet:

How to determine
if it is a "Pool" or a "Bay"

To help you decide if it is a "Pool" situation, link all the dots surrounding the space, starting on the last mesh of the horizontal row (dot shown with a gray center).

IF YOU CAN FORM A RING AROUND THE EMPTY SPACE,
YOU HAVE A "POOL" SITUATION.

This is a "Pool"
USE KEY No. 4

IF THE LINK DOES NOT CLOSE,
YOU HAVE A "BAY" SITUATION.

This is a "Bay"
USE KEYS No. 2 and No. 3

1. Because it is a "Pool" you do not complete the horizontal row immediately.
2. Go ahead in the left direction, making a Hidden Stitch on the loop of the vertical row* (under the empty mesh) to hide the thread while reaching the other dot.

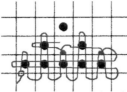

3. Complete the horizontal row. Notice that it goes from Right to Left, but because there are no more dots to be done, you draw the *Return* on the row.

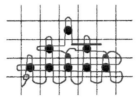

4. Change Direction to do the vertical row located over the empty mesh. Then you find yourself in the middle of the empty mesh.
5. On the next horizontal row, notice that you have just one thread in this horizontal row (the go-ahead thread). To have a complete row, we need 2 parallel lines. So, from where you are in the middle of the empty space, draw the *Return* on the row (bold upper line on illustration). This will complete the row that was already started.
6. You have now completed this small "Pool".

Depending on the pattern, sometimes the vertical row has not yet been done. Instead of using a Hidden Stitch, simply draw a vertical row (complete with the parallel Return – Key No. 2). See for an example "Exercise 6 - Tulip" and "Exercise 10 - Bird from the Bayeux tapestry".

1. Because it is a "Bay" situation, you do complete the parallel *Return* on the row (Key No.2)

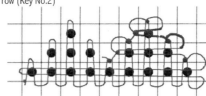

2. Make a Hidden Stitch to reach the other (one-mesh) horizontal row (which is also a "Bay" situation).
3. Complete this one-mesh row.
4. Then draw as many Hidden Stitches as necessary (5) to reach the other 3-mesh row to be completed (Key No.3).

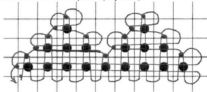

5. Now complete this cluster of dots, combined with the Hidden Stitches, until the Temporary knot is reached.

If you look at the patterns in Level 2, you will find many examples of "Bay" situations.

THE EMBROIDERY ON THE FILET NET

The sequence *Over* and *Under* is always the same on the filet net.

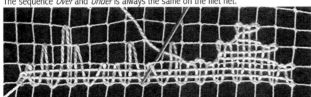

Someone I know made a drastic move: On a sheet of paper, she drew a large arrow pointing to the left with the words "HORIZONTAL – RIGHT to LEFT -- POOL" written just over it. It sure helped her to remember the 4th key; and I could hear her say... "Hands up...
Let's see ... Pool Situation?
...Yyyyessss
... Hidden Stitch"!!
..next situation now."

MULTIPLE "POOLS"

"Pools" come in a variety of shapes and sizes. Each "Pool" situation must be evaluated independently. Each time you draw a horizontal row from right to left and meet an empty mesh, it is one independent unit.

You have to determine if it is a "Pool "or a "Bay" situation each time you start to draw a "Horizontal-Row-Going-From-Right-to-Left". When you continue to the left, still horizontally, and meet another empty space, it becomes a potential "Pool or Bay" situation. Follow this illustrated path as we discover each situation independently:

1. This pattern has 2 "Pools". Can you see them?

2. Draw the path using Keys 1, 2 and 3, until you arrive at the Horizontal-Row- Going-from-Right-To-Left.

3. You are going horizontally to the left and you have an empty mesh on the left. Stop and evaluate the situation.

4. Begin joining the dots starting with the last dot on your horizontal row, just before the empty mesh. Go down to the next dot, and all around to form a ring.

5. Because the dots can be joined, it forms an enclosure. So it is a "Pool" situation (Key No. 4).

6. Draw a Hidden Stitch on the tip of this vertical row and continue your way to the left with the other horizontal row.
You have just done the first part of the "Pool" situation. You will return later to finish the *Return* on the row.

7. With this new horizontal row, you find yourself in a new situation to be evaluated.

8. This horizontal row, still going to the left, has an empty mesh on its left.

9. Can you join the dots?
Yes!
This is a "Pool" Situation.

10. So, draw a Hidden Stitch and continue to the left.
Look at the end of this series "Without using Key No. 4" and see the difference.

11. Because there is no more mesh to be done on the left, draw the *Return* on the row (Key No. 2).

12. Complete the other horizontal row.

13. Change direction to complete the vertical row.

Do you see that you are going around the "Pool", returning to the first point of entry where there is the half horizontal row?

14. Draw the horizontal row (this row goes from left to right, so use Key No. 2).

Then complete the mesh with the *Return* on the horizontal row (the row on which you started Key No. 4). By doing the *Return* on this mesh, the "Pool" is closed.

15. You have completed one "Pool" Situation. But remember, you still have to complete the one started earlier.

Look back at illustration 5.

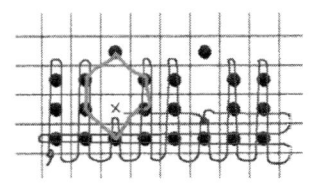
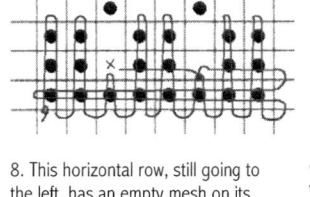
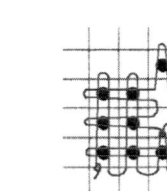
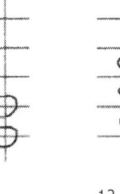
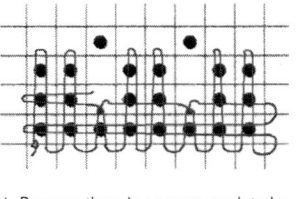

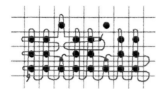

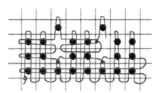

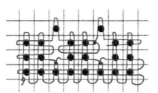

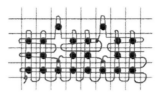

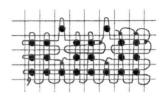

16. Draw a Hidden stitch to reach the vertical row.

17. Key No. 2: always complete the *Return* on the row.

18. Draw the horizontal row. You can see that this row is horizontal, but goes from left to right, so you apply Key No. 2: Always complete the *Return* on the row.

19. You now arrive where you have started the "Pool" Situation. After going around the "Pool", you now must complete the *Return* on the row.
This second "Pool" Situation is now completed.

20. Reach the next row with 3 Hidden Stitches.

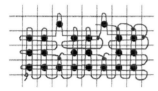

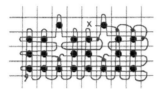

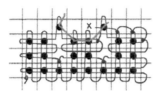

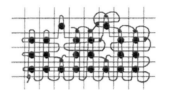

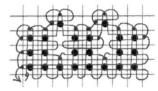

21. Draw a horizontal row. This row goes from right to left ...

22. ... and it has an empty mesh on its left.

23. Let's see if it is a "Pool" Situation: are the dots forming a ring? No. So it is a "Bay" Situation. Apply Key No. 2 ...always complete the *Return* on the row.

24. Use 4 Hidden Stitches to reach the other part on the pattern (Key No. 3) and draw a horizontal row.

25. Then make 7 Hidden Stitches to reach the Temporary knot and your pattern is complete.

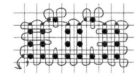

HOW TO DRAW THE HIDDEN STITCH WITH KEY NO. 4

WHAT WILL HAPPEN WITHOUT USING KEY No. 4

Redraw the path on this pattern without using Key No. 4: you will conclude that there is no way to reach the middle of the path. It is easy to imagine in a very large pattern that only borders of the design would be done.

1. Draw the first part of the horizontal row and take extra care to slightly pass the line.
2. Draw the little hook* to reach the tip of the loop.
3. Fill the tip with a Hidden Stitch.
4. And draw the next horizontal line to the left.

* Why a little hook? For faster reading. The little hook will speed the reading of the pattern while doing the embroidery on the filet net.

Mermie has a little secret :

Now, each time you draw from right to left and you are not sure if it is a "Pool" situation or a "Bay "situation, use Key No. 4 to do a "Pool" situation.

If you make a mistake, it is easier to transform a "Pool" situation where a "Bay" situation should apply. The "Bay" situation's mistake will not show so easily.

EXERCISES – POOL AND BAY

Reproduce each pattern on your graph paper and draw the path with the help of the illustration below. Then redo the path until you can make it without help, referring only to the definition of the Keys.

EXERCISE 1 – ENTRE-DEUX TRIM

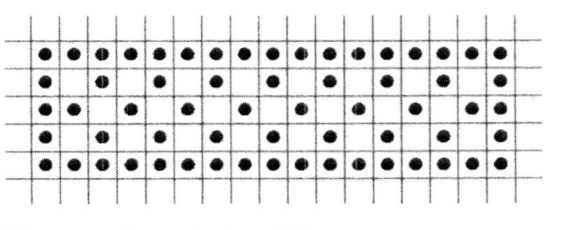 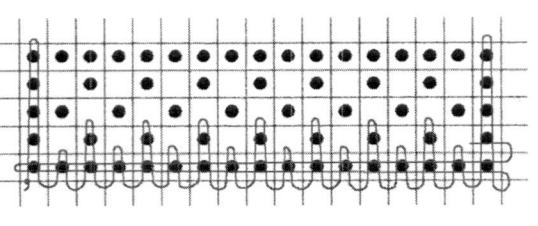 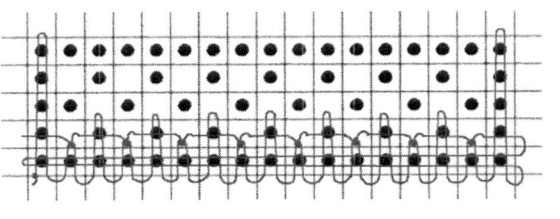

This pattern can be reproduced to make it longer.

Complete all the rows until you start working horizontally from right to left.

As you can see, these are all "Pool" situations. Each time you are working horizontally, verify if the empty mesh is well surrounded.

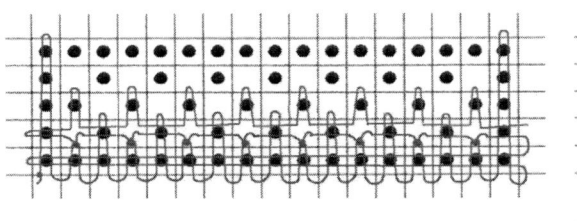 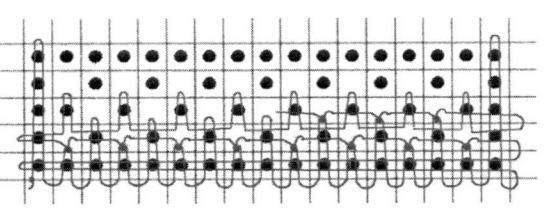 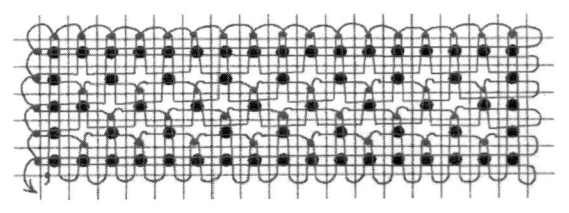

Do the *Returns* on the row using the vertical rows.

Continue on the other rows until you finish the last full row.

Reach the Temporary knot with Hidden Stitches.

EXERCISE 2 – TRIANGULAR BORDER

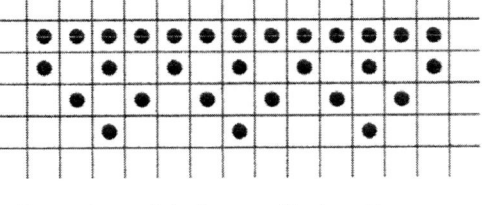 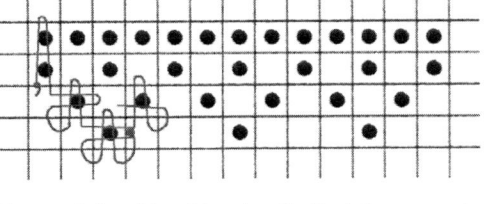 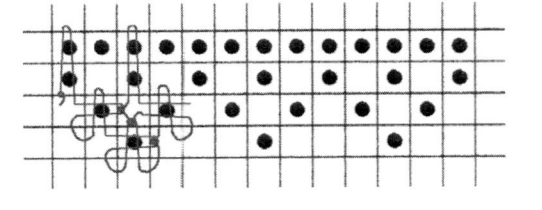

This pattern can be repeated to form a small border or trim.

Work horizontally from right to left, and use Key No. 4 since you can draw a ring around this empty space.

Then turn around the "Pool" and come back to complete the *Return* on the row.
In this example you do a Hidden Stitch on the left loop because the loop is already there.

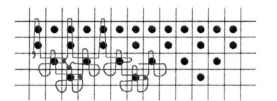

Continue tracing the path until you arrive at another horizontal row.
Verify the situation.

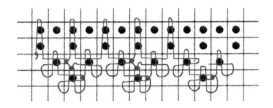

Another "Pool".

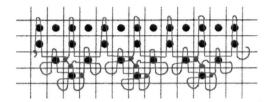

Here, you have several little "Pool" Situations.

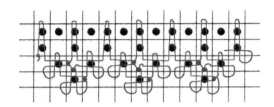

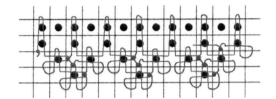

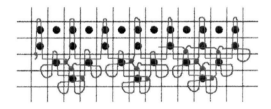

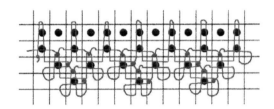

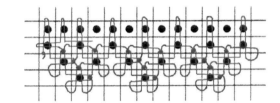

At this time, draw all the *Returns* on each one of the "Pool" situations using the vertical rows just over each empty mesh.

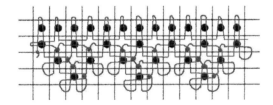

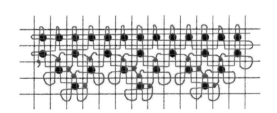

Then complete the last long horizontal row

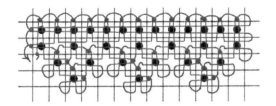

Use the Hidden Stitch to reach the Temporary knot and close your work with a Permanent knot in the middle of the vertical row.

EXERCISE 3 – HEART SHAPE

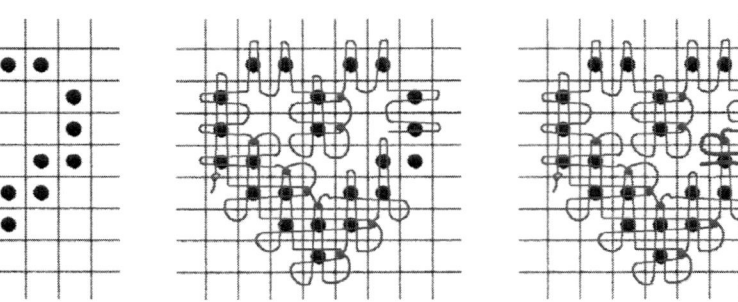

EXERCISES 4 – BORDER WITH INSIDE PICOTS

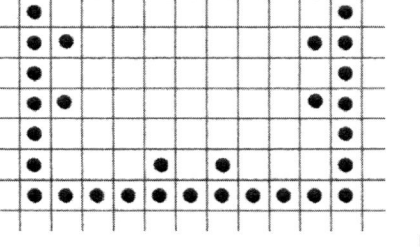

Key No. 4: ... starting a horizontal row from right to left

EXERCISE 5 – LEAF

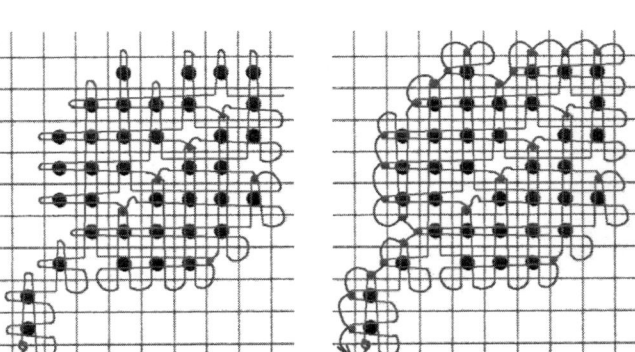

EXERCISE 6 — TULIP

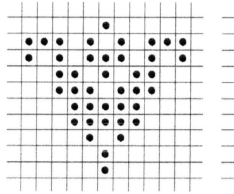 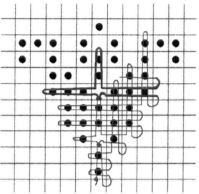 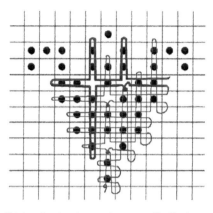 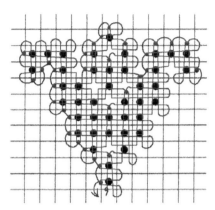

This is a situation where you have to use Key No. 4.
But there is no loop to apply a Hidden Stitch. You draw
the vertical row.

EXERCISE 7 — CENTRAL MOTIF

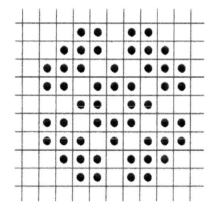 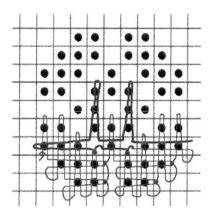 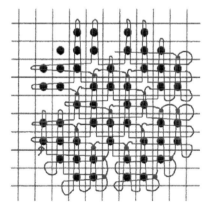 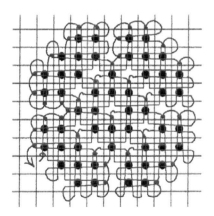

EXERCISE 8 — FLEUR DE LYS FROM THE BAYEUX TAPESTRY

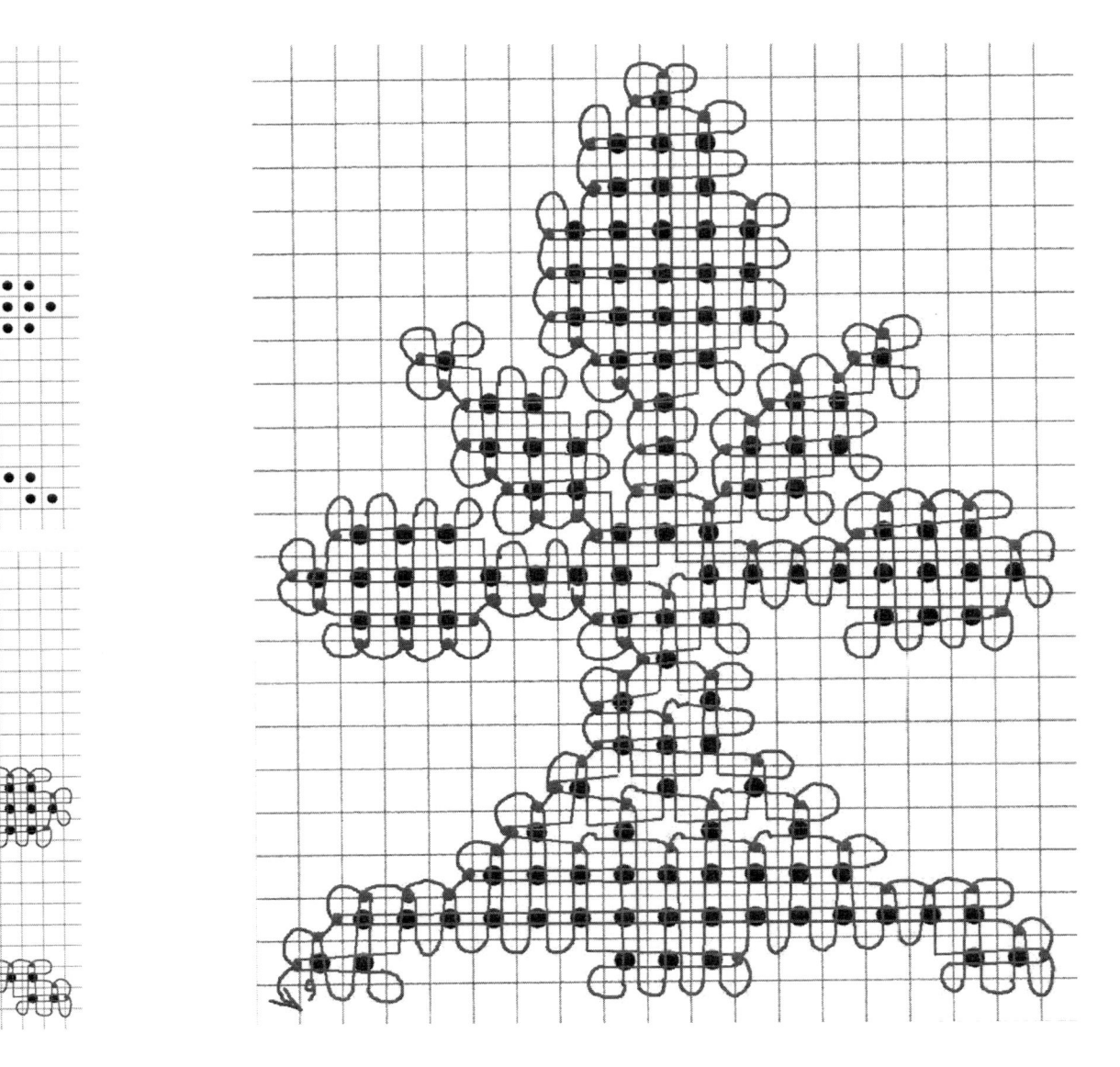

EXERCISE 9 – COAT OF ARMS

We are dealing with a serious pattern. All these intricate openings in the pattern must be avoided using Key No. 4. This is a very good exercise. It has small intricate "Pools". Go slowly. Straight lines and well- proportioned loops will help you.

Study the path already done on the right. Then hide it. Try to draw this path without looking at the completed pattern until you can do it by yourself.

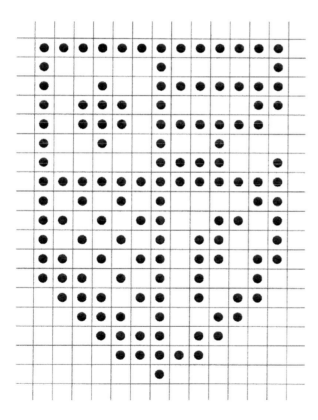

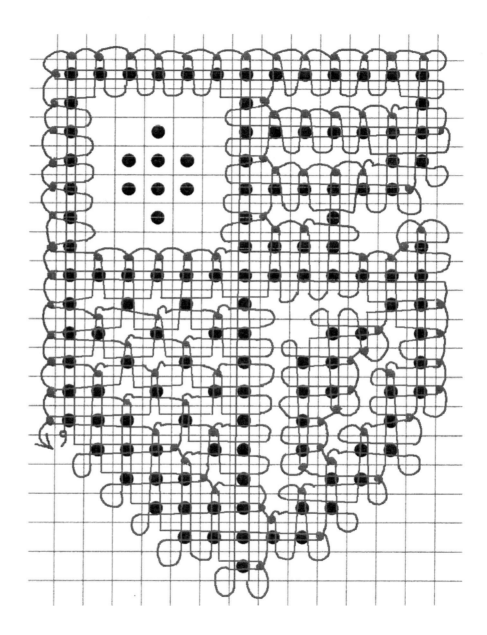

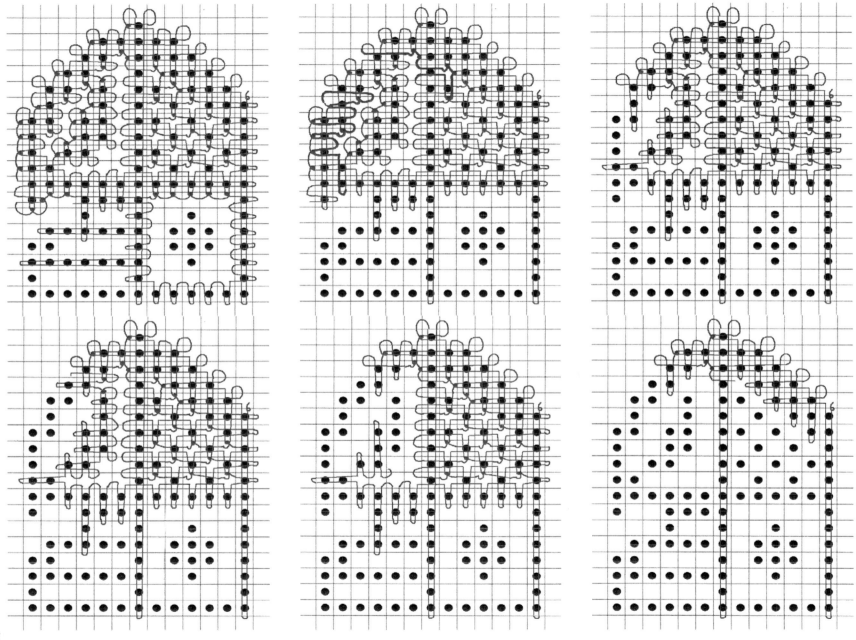

EXERCICE 10 – BIRD FROM THE BAYEUX TAPESTRY

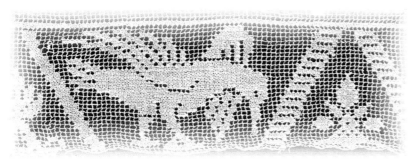

Photo No. 18 – Detail in the Bayeux tapestry border

This exercise will require more patience and determination. So far, you have learned all the necessary tools to achieve it. 'Practice' is the only thing missing. A note though: you could be tempted to use the Key No. 4 in all directions, going up or going to the right; Sure, it can be done! But not now, as it will be confusing to add more to your new knowledge and limited experience. So, remain with the Keys.   Later, you may want to do it for esthetic reasons, but not yet as it will slow your learning and will confuse you at this stage.

Carefully follow the instructions, do not anticipate too far ahead, and do not worry.

Draw your lines straight and your loops in the proper proportions. Apply a nice big dot at the tip of the loop for the Hidden stitch. Follow the finishing path and study highlights on the other patterns. Then, with the page describing the Keys in front of you, start doing the path by yourself. If you become lost, erase the whole thing and begin again. Do not press too hard on your pencil!!

This pattern is 31 meshes x 48 meshes.

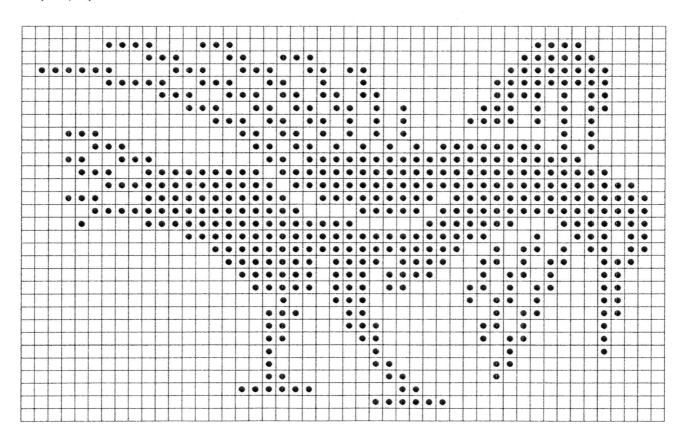

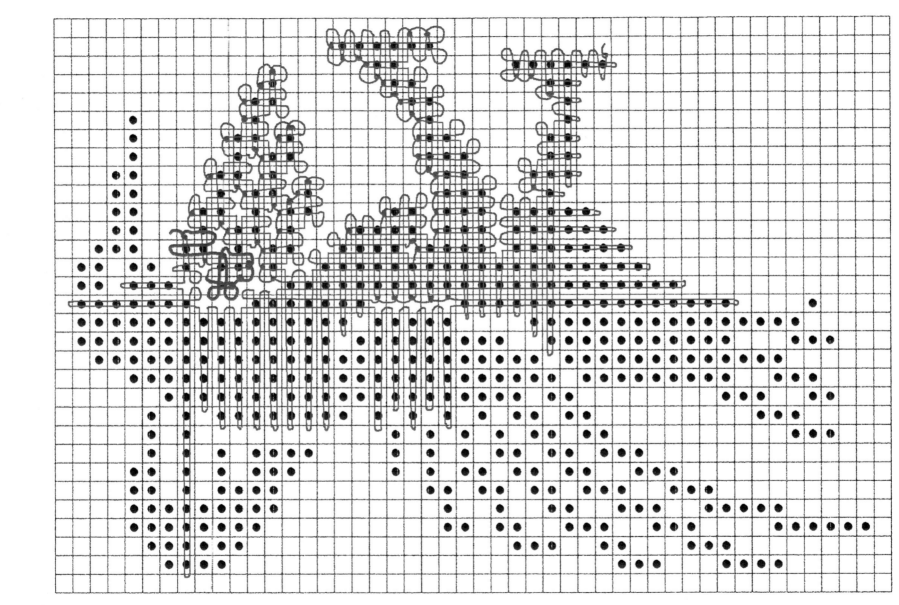

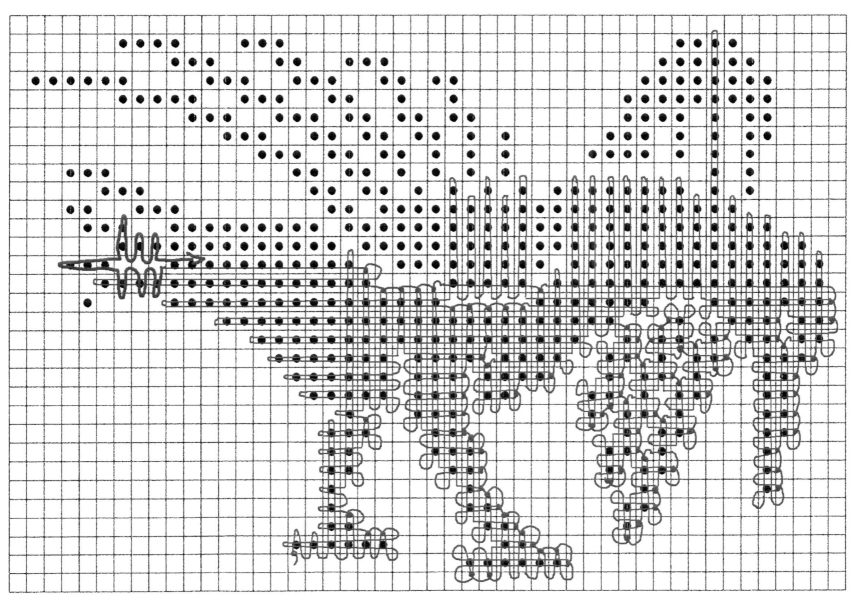

We use Key No. 4 with a Hidden Stitch to go around "Pools". When there is no existing loop to apply a Hidden Stitch, we complete the vertical row (do not forget to always complete the *Return* on the vertical row-Key No. 2).

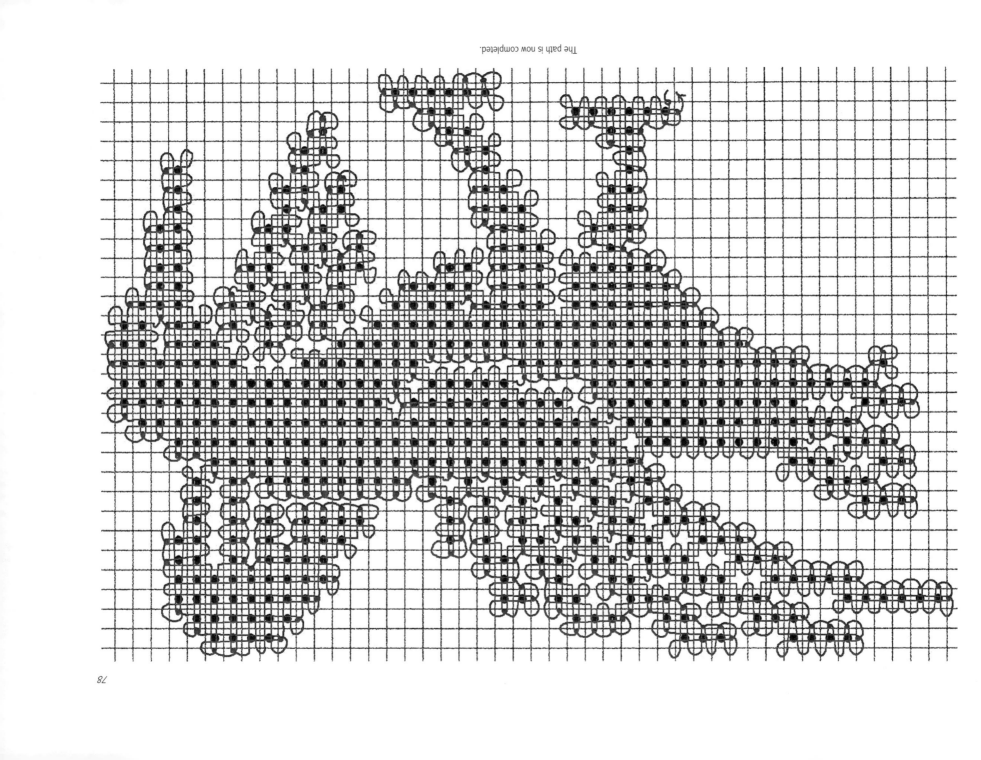

REVIEW LEVEL 3 – POOL AND BAY

THE ULTIMATE TSUNAMI

Speak the Direction & Keys out loud as they appear. Take your time and watch for Key No. 4. You have been erasing often over the last few pages ... but do not be discouraged. Be persistent and you will make it through the storm.

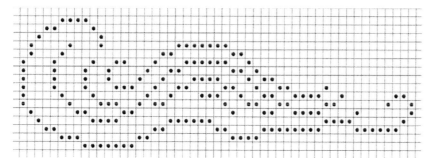
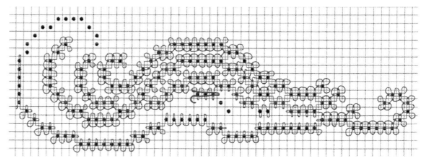

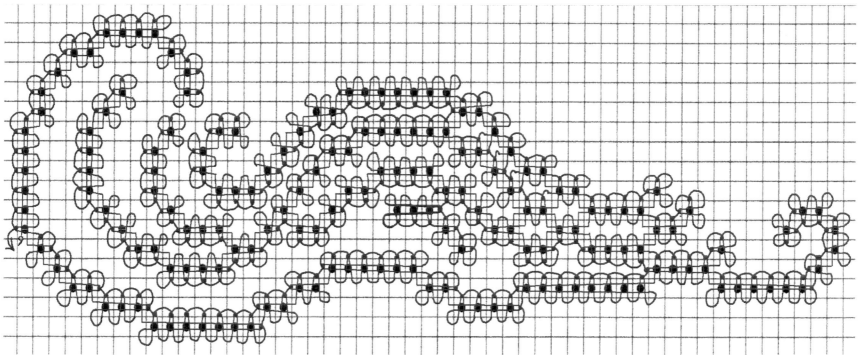

1st PROJECT – LEVEL 3
The well-cut doily – Simplified
Linen Stitch and Buttonhole Stitch

The pattern is 41 x 41 meshes. When finished it measures 7.50" x 7.25".

This pattern has been separated into 17 smaller shapes to make it easier for everyone with limited experience to do an interesting piece of lace. The path is easier to draw because of the smaller sections. On the embroidery, you will have learned how to start at the right place and how to make the knots. The full pattern, as it should be, follows as the second project for Level 3.

The big dots are the meshes to be filled with the Linen Stitch; the Buttonhole Stitch for the border is done on the lines; and the filet net is cut following the smaller dots.

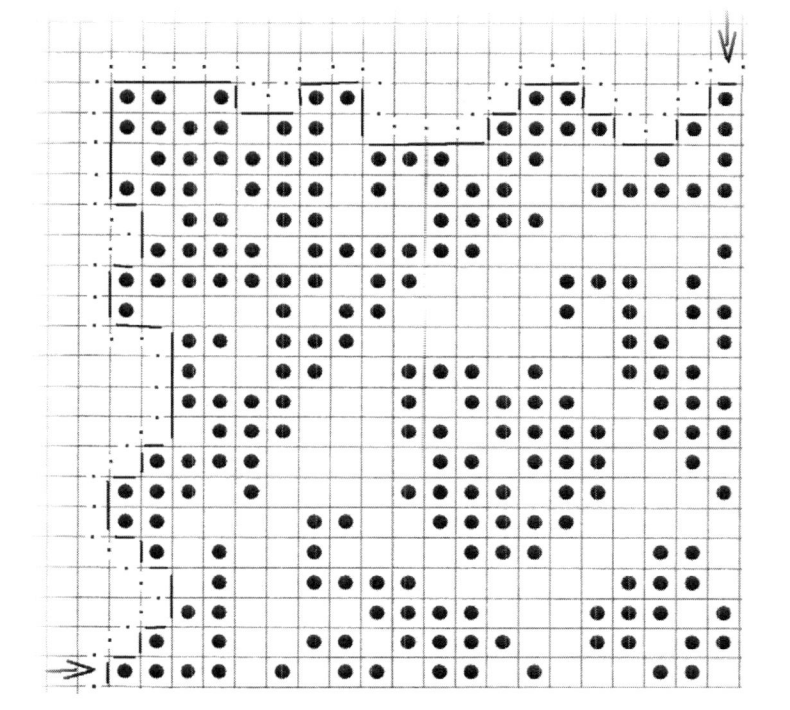

MATERIAL

Filet Net 5 to fit your embroidery frame
10 grams of Coton Perlé DMC No. 5 ecru

PATTERN

1. Reproduce this pattern 4 times; the arrows mark the middle row of the pattern (do not reproduce the small dots or the lines: only the large dots).
2. Draw the path using Keys No. 1, 2, 3 and 4.
3. When completely done, trace over the pencil marks with a light colored gel pen; erase the pencil marks and prepare to start the embroidery on the filet net.

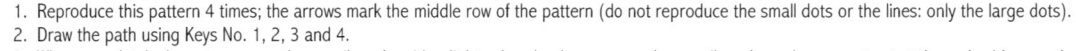

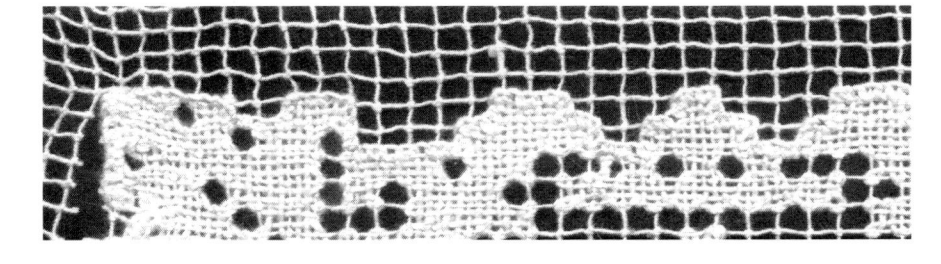
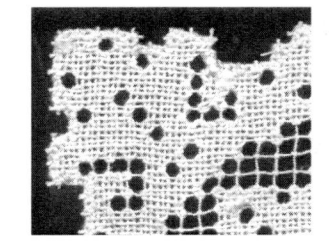

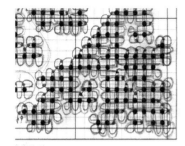

This corner motif has been followed with a pencil while doing the embroidery.

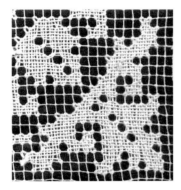

EMBROIDERY ON THE FILET NET

4. Place your pattern on the table and follow it a bit at a time, with your pencil on the pattern.
5. Prepare your needle with 4 yards of thread each time.
6. Start with the corner motif on the left.
7. Then with another 4 yards, do one entre-deux triangular motif, one leaf and one flower.
8. Start the Buttonhole Stitch in the middle of one side and follow the cutting line.
9. Cut the filet leaving ¼" after the small knot of the filet net.
10. Wash and / or bleach your lace.
11. Block it on the ironing board, iron in place and allow to dry.

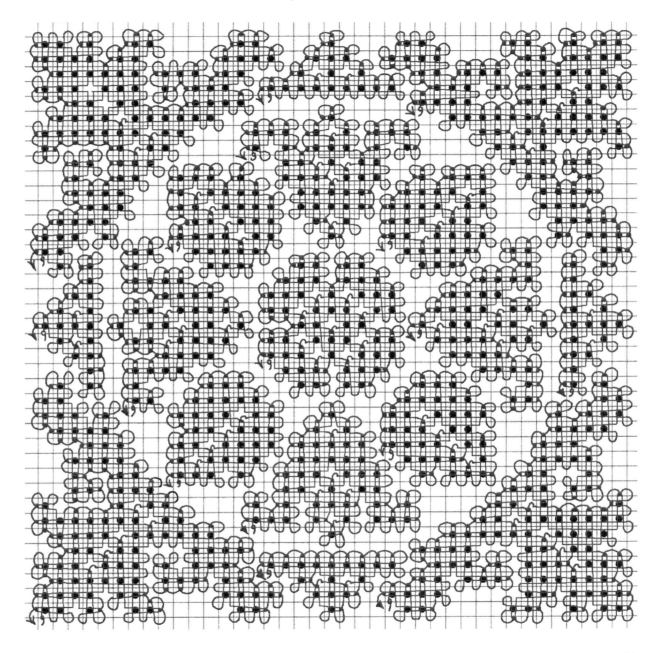

2nd PROJECT – LEVEL 3
The well-cut doily – Regular pattern
Linen Stitch and Buttonhole

This pattern is 39 meshes x 39 meshes.

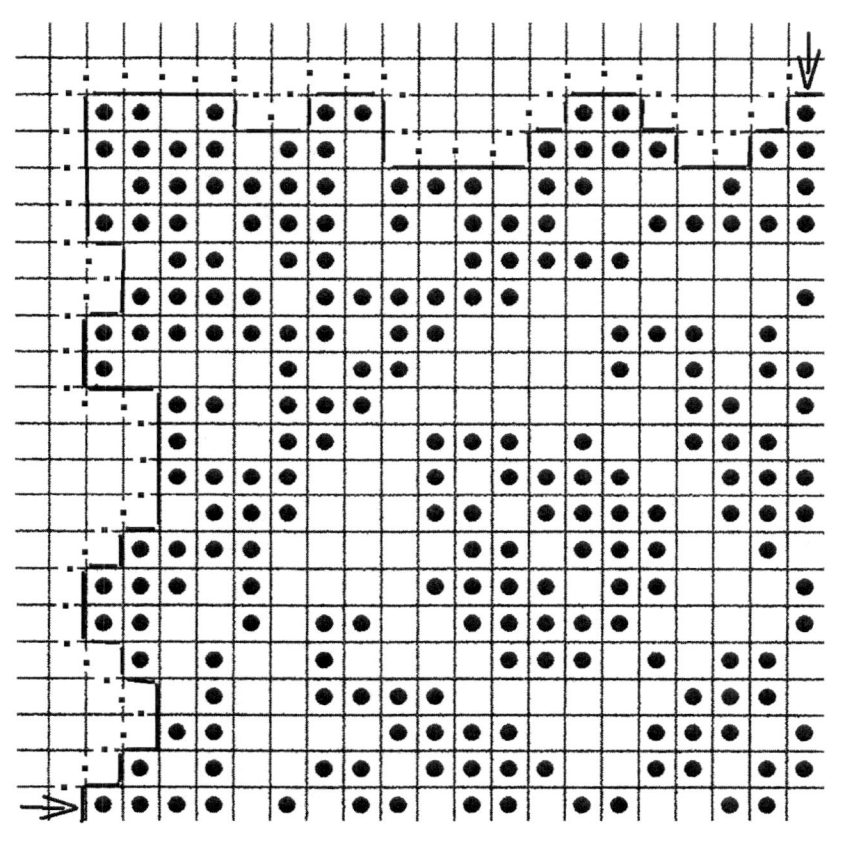

Reproduce this portion of the pattern 4 times to form the entire pattern (do not reproduce the small dots or the lines: only the large dots).

This is the pattern as it should be: with as few knots as possible. It will require more patience in doing the path.

The project has 2 shapes: the border and the center motif. The path of this border has been done using Key No. 4. It can also be done like the border of the project in Level 2 (you do the outside first and then turn and do the inside).

As the center motif is not part of the border (because the dots are not touching), the center becomes a large "Pool". As soon as you are working Horizontally-from-Right-to-Left, use Key No. 4 (look at the picture below for the general direction for this border).

Reproduce this path on your Filet Net No. 5 using Coton Perlé DMC No. 5, with 6 yards of thread at a time. Finish the edges with a Buttonhole Stitch following the straight lines on the quarter pattern produced at left. Cut your lace at the small dots. Wash and bleach your lace. Block it on the ironing board, iron in place and allow to dry.

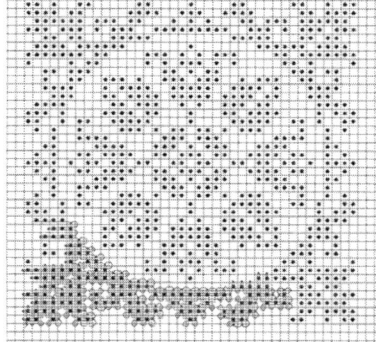
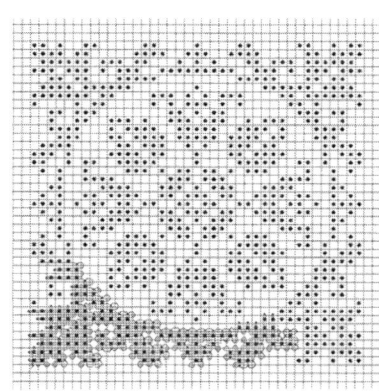

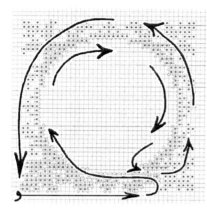

GENERAL VIEW FOR THE DIRECTION OF THIS BORDER USING KEY No. 4:

This border is One shape. The path of the border is done using Key No. 4: "... start working horizontally, from right to left..." the center is like a big "Pool". The illustration shows you, in general, how the path proceeds when using this Key.

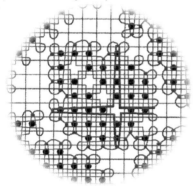

THIS IS ALSO KEY No. 4:

This is another situation where there is no loop to do a Hidden Stitch. In order to bypass the "Pool" Situation, simply draw the vertical row going down.

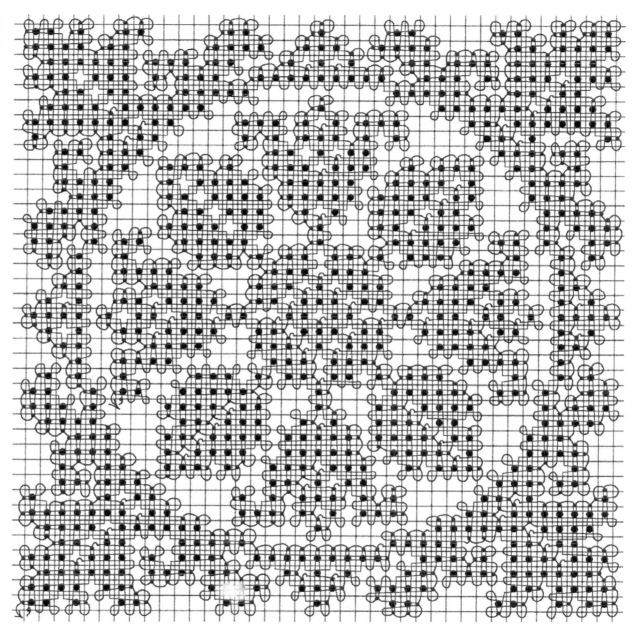

Congratulations!

You are now ready to start a larger project by yourself.
Choose a pattern in the next chapter; or maybe you already have books of patterns.

In the mean time, continue doing "paths" regularly.
Your next goal is to improve your calligraphy and gain speed.
I can't wait to see your future curtains!!

Good Luck !

Mermie

CHAPTER 6
MORE PATTERNS

Bank of Patterns
Go online and
visit Filet Lace
By The Sea for
more beautiful
patterns adapted
for Filet Lace
technique. Bank of
Patterns Filet
Lace Introduction
to the Linen
Stitch

LET THE ADVENTURE BEGIN

Practice your "Paths" with these patterns adapted for your level. They are inspired from my collection of antique books and lace. Open your own books on counted stitch patterns and find more ideas.

You can transform these patterns to produce doilies, trim for hand towels, bed sheets or edgings on curtains. You can also create pillow cases, tapestries or pieces to be framed, as well as curtains of all sizes.

To prepare the pattern, calculate the meshes needed for the size of your project. On your graph paper reproduce the size in meshes, add the chosen motif and add an interesting border. You can add silk ribbon, beads, fringe, small tassels, etc. to your creations.

The measurement of your finished filet lace depends on the size of the mesh. Filet Net 3 has 3 meshes per inch and Filet Net 5 has 5 meshes per inch. To calculate the finished size of the chosen pattern, you divide the number of meshes by 3 when using Filet Net 3 and by 5 if you are using Filet Net 5. To calculate the number of meshes in a 12-inch project, multiply by 3 when using Filet Net 3 and by 5 for Filet Net 5.

The white line on the edges of some patterns is the place where the filet is cut after having done the Buttonhole stitch.

For more choices and ideas go online to www.filetlace.net.

PATTERN INDEX

FILET LACE - INTRODUCTION TO THE LINEN STITCH

No. 1   No. 2   No. 3   No. 4   No. 5   No. 6   No. 7

No. 9   No. 10   No. 11   No. 12   No. 13   No. 17   No. 16   No. 19

No. 21   No. 22   No. 23

No. 8   No. 15   No. 14

No. 24   No. 20   No. 18   No. 25

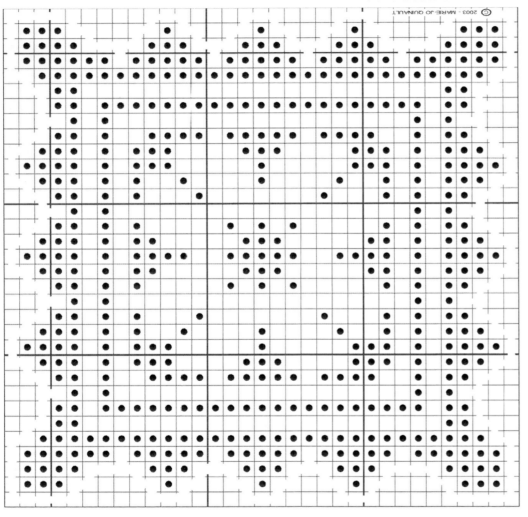

Pattern No. 1 – BORDERS (for Level 2)

© 2003 - MARIE-JO QUINAULT

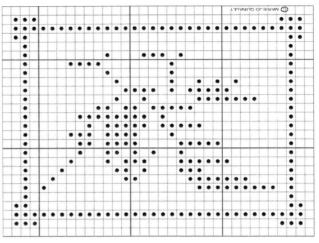

Pattern No. 5 – BABY BIRD (Easy for Level 3)

© MARIE-JO QUINAULT

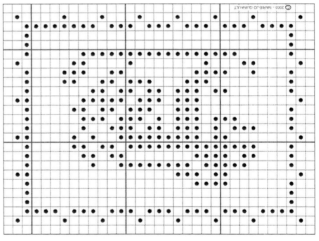

Pattern No. 6 – FROG (Easy for level 3)

© 2003 - MARIE-JO QUINAULT

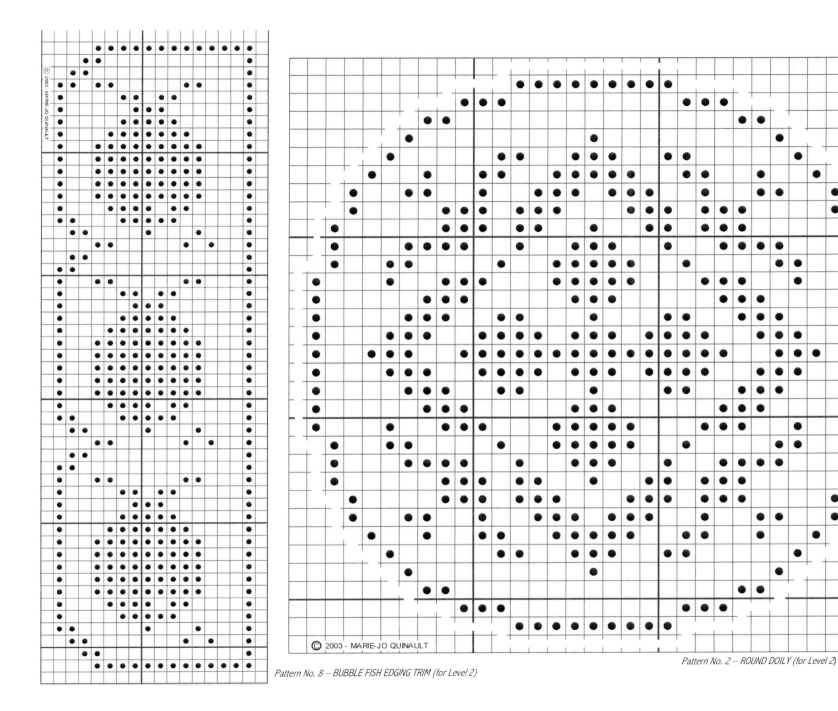

Pattern No. 8 – BUBBLE FISH EDGING TRIM (for Level 2)

Pattern No. 2 – ROUND DOILY (for Level 2)

89

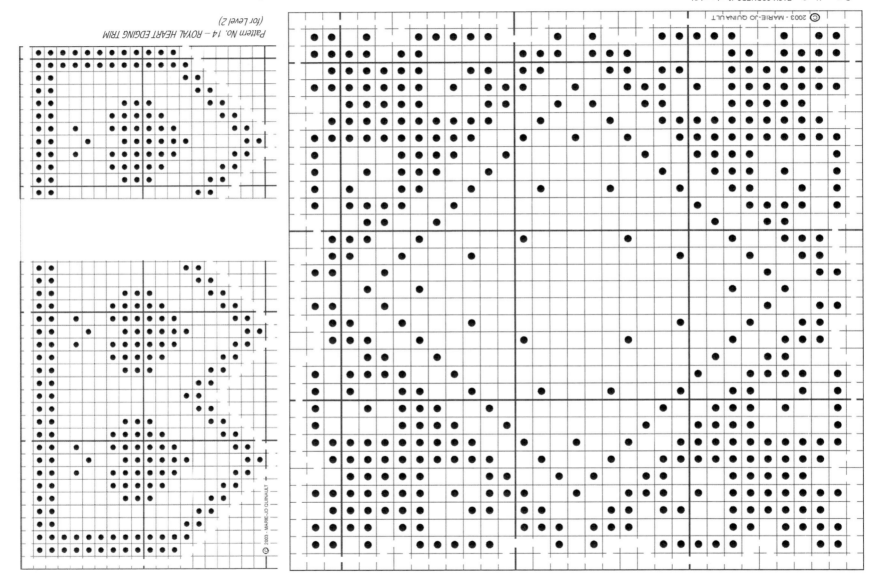

Pattern No. 3 – EASY CORNERS (for Level 2)

© 2003 - MARIE-JO QUINAULT

Pattern No. 14 – ROYAL HEART EDGING TRIM (for Level 2)

© 2003 - MARIE-JO QUINAULT

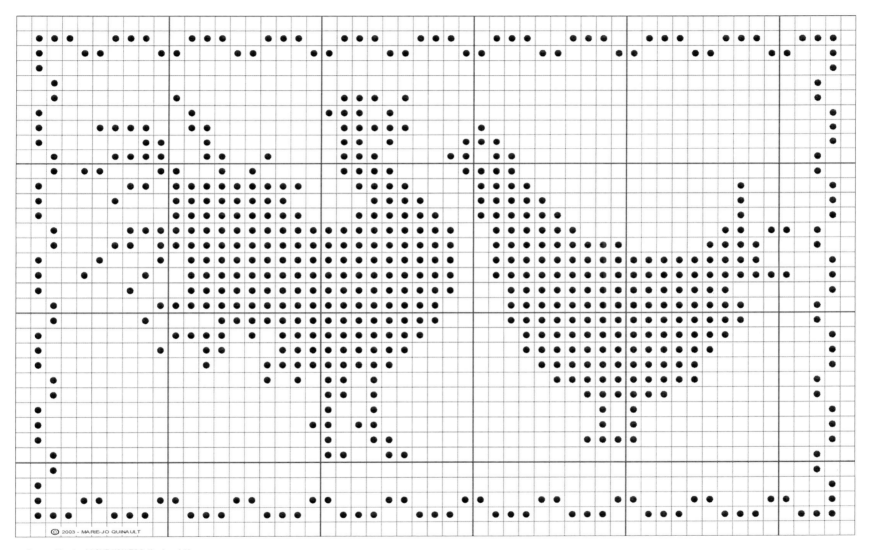

Pattern No. 4 – *I LOVE YOU TOO (for Level 2)*

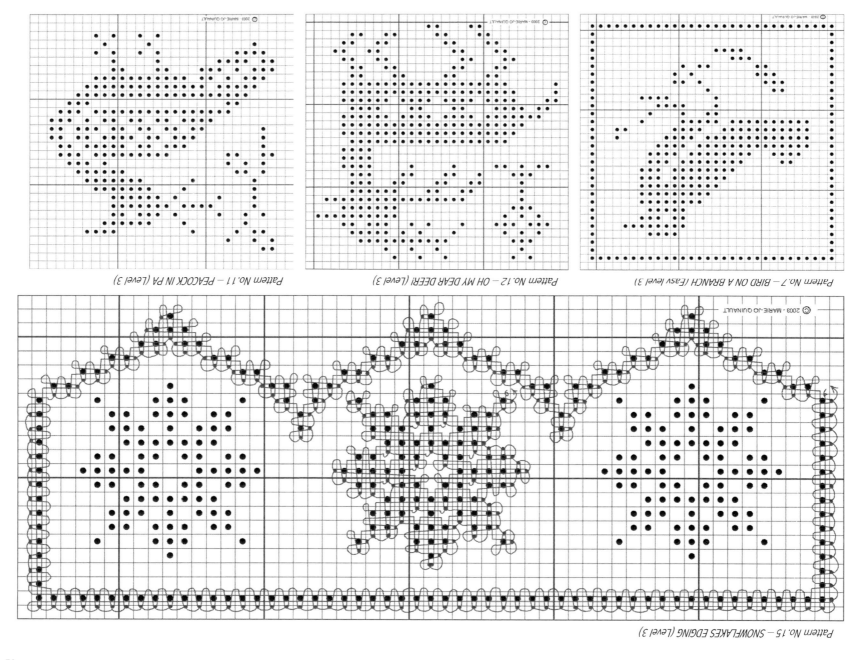

Pattern No.11 — PEACOCK IN PA (Level 3)

Pattern No.12 — OH MY DEAR DEER! (Level 3)

Pattern No.7 — BIRD ON A BRANCH (Easy level 3)

Pattern No.15 — SNOWFLAKES EDGING (Level 3)

© 2003 - MARIE-JO QUINAULT

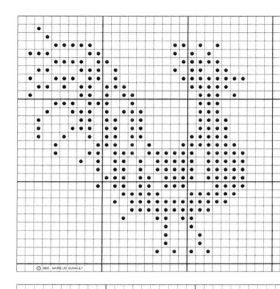

Pattern No.10 – LE COQUART-DIT (Level3)

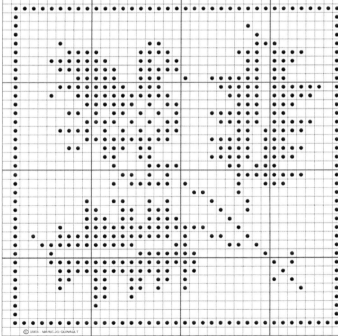

Pattern No.9 – BABY BIRD ON AN OAK (Level 3)

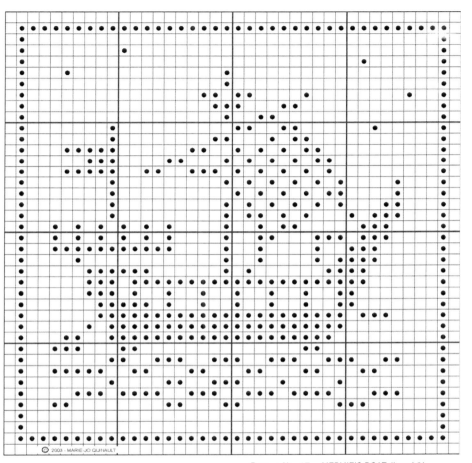

Pattern No. 17 – MERMIE'S BOAT (Level 3)

Pattern No. 20 – DOILY VICTORIA (Level 3)

Pattern No.18 – THE CORAL CASTLE (Level 3)

Pattern No.19 – DOILY TULIPS (Level 3)

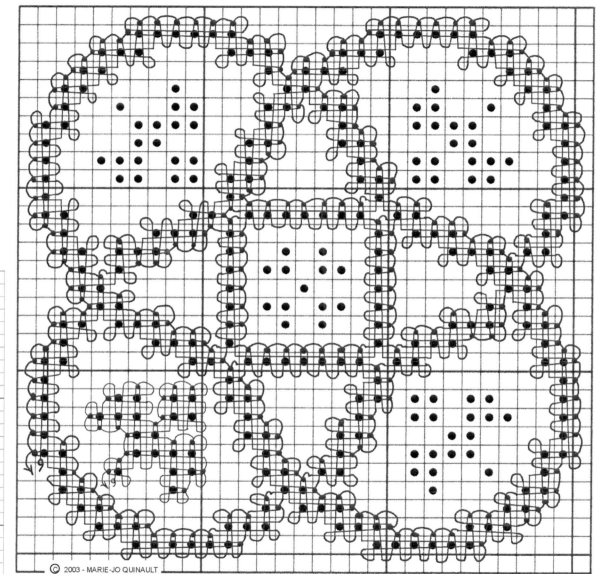

Pattern No.16 —EASY DOILY WITH ROUND CORNERS (Level 3)

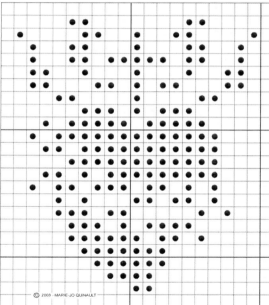

Pattern No.13 — FOR CHURCH LINEN (Level 3)

© 2003 - MARIE-JO QUINAULT

© 2003 - MARIE-JO QUINAULT

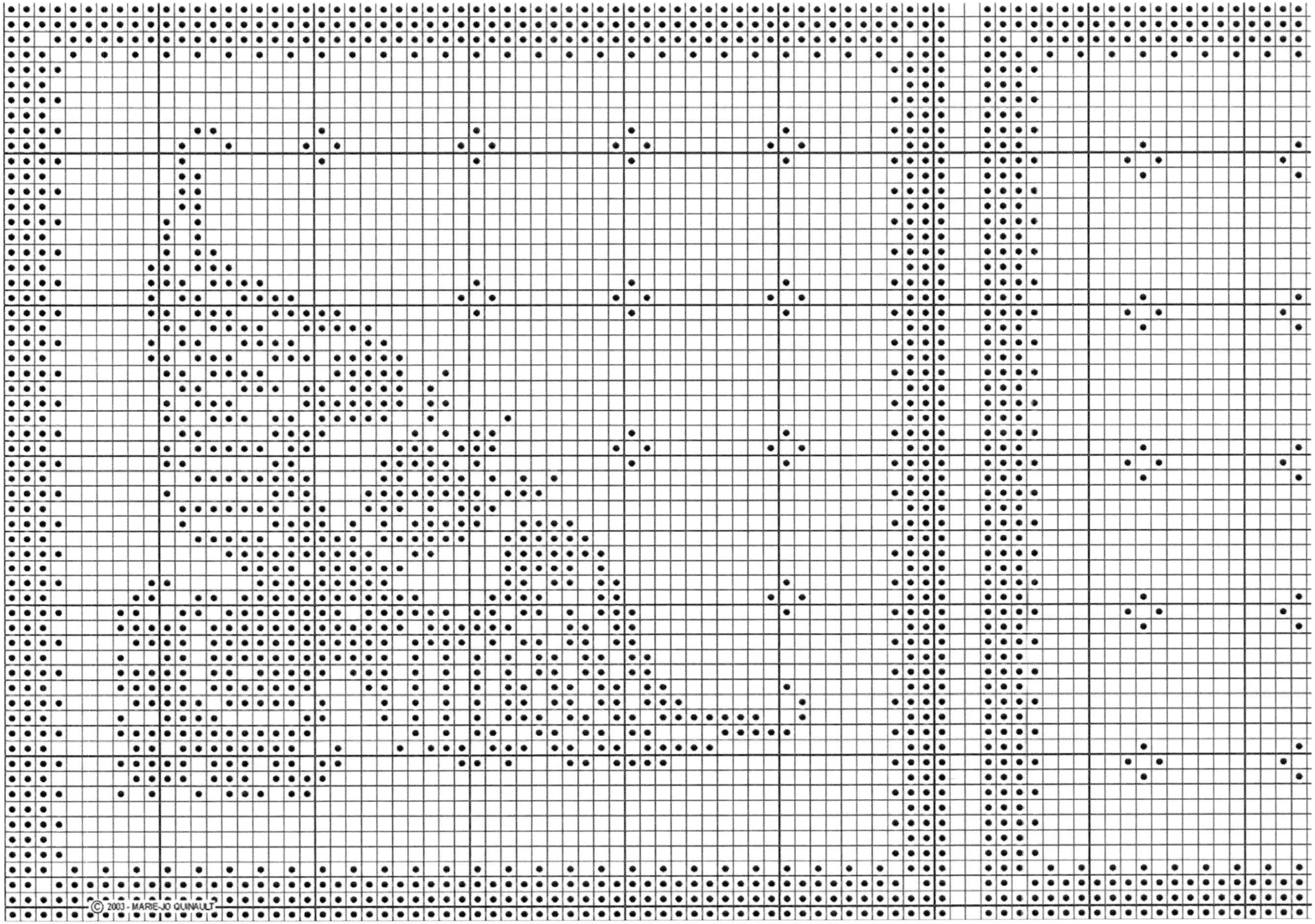
© 2003 - MARIE-JO QUINAULT

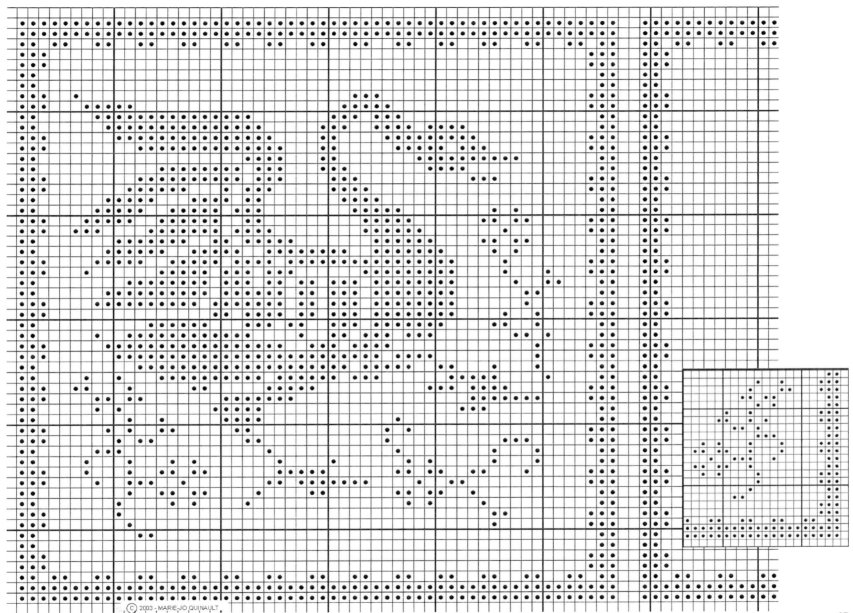

Pattern No.22 – THE GOOSE, PILLOW TOP AND BACK (Level 3)

© 2003 - MARIE-JO QUINAULT

Pattern No.23 – MERMIE, PILLOW TOP AND BACK (Level 3)

Pattern No 24 –
CINDERELLA
(Level 3)

Pattern No.25 – EASY CURTAIN WITH REPETITIVE MOTIF (Easy-Level 3 for the motif but Advanced-Level 3 because of the size)

BON VOYAGE!

REFERENCES & CREDITS

"Renaissance Patterns for Lace, Embroidery and Needlepoint, Federico Vinciolo - an unabridged facsimile of the "Singuliers et nouveaux pourtraicts" of 1587",
Dover publications New York (1971)

"Le Filet Ancien au Point de Reprise No. 6"
Wolf & Dupeyron Editeurs (April 1920)

"Le Filet Ancien au Point de Reprise No. 9"
Wolf & Dupeyron Editeurs (November 1921)

"Le Filet Brodé — 114 modèles"
Imprimerie Paul Dupont, Paris (around 1900)

"The technique of Filet Lace"
Pauline Knight
BT Batsford Limited, London (1980)

"Encyclopédie des Ouvrages de Dames"
Thérèse de Dillmont
Editions Th. De Dillmont, Mulhouse, France
(First published in 1886)

"Dentelle sur Filet Noue"
Annevan de Vegue
Editions Héritage, Montréal (1982)

"Rope, Twine and Net making"
Anthony Sanctuary
Shire Publications Ltd (1996)

"Borders, frames & decorations of the art nouveau period"
Edited by Carol Belanger Grafton

"Art Nouveau motifs and vignettes"
Selected and arranged by Carol Belanger Grafton

Credits for Lace

Ruth YOUNGBLOOD
THE BLUE RIDGE MOUNTAIN
LACEMAKER'S GUILD
Waynesboro, Pennsylvania, USA
lovelylace@earthlink.net
Page 6 — Photo no. 6

Olga YAKUNINA
OLGA YAKUNINA LADA WORKSHOP
Samara, Russia
www.ssu.samara.ru/~lada/eng
Page 6 — Photo no. 7

Marie-Jo QUINAULT
FILET LACE BY THE SEA
Southwest Florida USA
www.filetlace.net
All other laces are from Marie-Jo's
private collection

Lace photo list

Photo 1 — Detail of Linen Stitch on Garden Gate Curtain
Photo 2 — Detail of the middle scene (Bayeux Tapestry)
Photo 3 — Rare panel of Filet Lace showing scenes based on the Bayeux Tapestry 58" x 14"
Photo 4 — Filet shuttle and gauge
Photo 5 — This is the old loom we are using to knot Filet Net 3 for FILET LACE BY THE SEA
Photo 6 — Peacock from an old German design embroidered in Linen Stitch on Filet Net 3
　　　　　by *Ruth Youngblood* — Detail of her curtain panel
Photo 7 — Filet-Guipure lace, contemporary lace (7"x7") created
　　　　　by *Olga Yakunina*
Photo 8 — Example of Filet-Richelieu, from Pauline Knight's book.
Photo 9 — The Unicorn: Pattern from F. Vinciolo 16th century executed by MJ Quinault
Photo 10 — Round collar, contemporary filet lace created by Marie-Jo Quinault
Photo 11 — Antique Baby bed cover 42"x42": Filet Lace and Cutwork embroidery. Author's col ection
Photo 12 — Detail in the Bayeux tapestry border
Photo 13 — Valance for a canopy bed
Photo 14 — Detail from the Antique baby bed cover
Photo 15 — Detail of a square from the Antique Baby Bed Cover
Photo 16 — Three motifs from the border of the Antique baby bed cover
Photo 17 — Detail of a square from the Antique baby bed cover
Photo 18 — Detail in the Bayeux tapestry border

ISBN 1-4150-2549-9